# SEVEN GUIDES TO LASTING LOVE

# Seven Guides to Lasting Love

**COLIN WHITTAKER**

**KINGSWAY PUBLICATIONS**
EASTBOURNE

ISBN 0 85476 853 X

Published by
KINGSWAY PUBLICATIONS
Lottbridge Dove, Eastbourne, BN23 6NT, England.
E-mail: books@kingsway.co.uk

Designed and produced for the publishers by
Bookprint Creative Services, P.O. Box 827, BN21 3YJ, England.
Printed in Great Britain.

# Contents

# Acknowledgements

My thanks are due to all my friends, family and colleagues who have helped me in the preparation of this book, but the following deserve my special thanks.

For their patience, advice and help in locating and obtaining books essential for my research, the Librarian and staff of Eastwood Library, and of Nottingham County Council Libraries.

The Officer in Charge of The Salvation Army Nottingham Goodwill Centre, William Booth Memorial Complex, 14 Notintone Place, Nottingham, NG2 4QG.

The Officer and staff of The Salvation Army Heritage Centre, 117–121 Judd Street, London, WC1H 9NN.

The Warden and staff of the Epworth Centre, Epworth Old Rectory (home of the Wesleys), 1 Rectory Street, Epworth, Doncaster, DN9 1HK.

Vernon Ralphs and Dr William Kay, faculty members of Mattersey Bible College, Mattersey, and Revd Dr Henry Rack of Manchester: all of whom found time in their busy lives to supply me with sources and guidance.

Last but above all, my dear wife Hazel – my most constructive critic and ever my greatest encourager.

# Introduction

I feel this introduction calls for an apology plus an explanation from me. I do not apologise for writing about these notables, but I do so for my temerity in including an autobiographical section along with the stories of these great believers. My explanation is that I know these are all extraordinary people. I also know only too well that I am just an ordinary person, which is why it has been included with the hope of showing that the lowliest of believers and servants of Christ can also be sure of receiving his unfailing help to build a loving, lasting marriage.

In his massive and marvellous autobiography *Just As I Am* Billy Graham with helpful and admirable Christian candour acknowledges:

Ruth and I don't have a perfect marriage, but we have a great one. How can I say two things that seem so contradictory? In a perfect marriage, everything is always the finest and best imaginable, like a Greek statue, the proportions are exact and the finish is unblemished. Who knows any human beings like that? For a married couple to expect perfection in each other is unrealistic. We learned that before we were married.

Being human, not one of us will ever have a relationship with another person that doesn't have a wrinkle or a wart on it some-where. The unblemished ideal exists only in 'happily ever after' fairytales. I think there is some merit to a description I once read of a married couple as 'happily incompatible.' Ruth likes to say, 'If two people agree on everything, one of them is unnecessary.' The sooner we accept that as a fact of life, the better we will be able to adjust to each other and enjoy togetherness. 'Happily incompatible' is a good adjustment.

At the funeral service of Princess Diana, millions of viewers and listeners were deeply moved as, with evident feeling, Prime Minister Tony Blair read the apostle Paul's description of love from 1 Corinthians 13. Here are some of those verses in a modern translation which are especially pertinent for all seeking to ensure they have a lasting, loving marriage:

Love is patient, love is kind. It does not envy, it does not boast, it is not proud. It is not rude, it is not self-seeking, it is not easily angered, it keeps no record of wrongs. Love does not delight in evil but rejoices with the truth. It always protects, always trusts, always hopes, always perseveres. Love never fails . . . (1 Corinthians 13:4–8).

Billy Graham's wife, Ruth, in her exquisitely tender book *It's My Turn* shares a story that beautifully illustrates this kind of love concerning her mother and father, distinguished mis-sionaries in China, he a gifted doctor and surgeon. In his later years Dr L. Nelson Bell served as Moderator of the Southern Presbyterian Church. Ruth writes:

Mother had had a stroke several years before which had left her confined to a wheelchair, with her speech slightly affected. . . . One morning when I dropped by to see how they were, I found Daddy on his knees in front of Mother, helping her put on her stockings. Daddy had reached the point where he got up and down with dif-ficulty. He, who had been an athlete in his younger days . . . now found himself with a painfully ulcerated toe that refused to heal due to the fact that he was a border-line diabetic and had lost circulation in his left leg. He glanced up at me over his glasses, giving me his usual broad smile of welcome. 'You know,' he said, returning to Mother's stocking, 'these are the happiest days of our lives. Caring for your mother is the greatest privilege of my life.' And the nice thing was, he meant it.

The idea for this book had its origin many years back after I had been invited to lecture on William Booth at an Assemblies of God Home Missions Conference. In researching the lives of William and Catherine I was moved to tears on reading about William's love for his beloved Catherine as she lay in agony, dying with cancer. I thought then, 'This is a true love story; how different to so many of the "romances" conjured up for TV.' And so it simmered over the years, never losing its fascination, with the discovery of more details of their love, which not even a deathbed could dim. That is the love God intended a man and a woman to have for each other.

Their son, Bramwell Booth, in his *Echoes and Memories*, quotes the words his father spoke beside Catherine's open grave: 'I have never turned from her these forty years for any journeyings on my mission of mercy, but I longed to get back, and have counted the weeks, days, and hours which should take me again to her side.'

Love never fails.

# 1

# *Martin and Katrina Luther*

It was 3rd April 1523. The nine young ladies were intent on maintaining the highest level of secrecy possible because the situation they were in was so dangerous. One by one, eight shadowy figures tiptoed down the stone-flagged passage under the welcome cover of the night. Each hugged the darker side of the long corridor, pausing after every few steps to listen and look over her shoulder lest they be discovered. Scarcely daring to breathe, they paused in turn at a small door, which – after the gentlest of taps – opened immediately.

Eventually, after more anxious moments, the last one arrived in Katrina's cell. Katrina (full name Katherine von Bora) was the one to whom they looked for leadership. All nine of these young women were of noble birth, and the cell in which they were meeting was in a convent not a prison – although it had become more and more like a prison, and escaping from it was just as difficult. For months, without a single ray of hope, they had been plotting to escape.

This convent of Cistercian nuns at Nimptschen (not far from Leipzig) was reserved for ladies of noble birth. Due to the increasing influence of Martin Luther the Reformation was growing stronger every day, and all nine of them had become convinced of the unlawfulness of their vows. They had written to their relatives and asked leave to return home, but none of the noble families was willing to face the ignominy that this would involve them in.

As a last resort, Katrina had said she would write to Martin Luther to see if he could help them. They had all heard of him – some of Luther's writings had found their way even into the convent where they had read them in secret. Indeed, it seemed that everyone in Germany was aware of this courageous monk who had defied the pope and the emperor in his stand for the much-needed reformation of the church.

One look at Katrina's eager young face (she was still only in her early twenties) and they knew she had news for them. When she told them that not only had the letter she had smuggled out got safely to Luther, but she had also received the great man's reply, they broke out in excited chatter. Katrina had to quieten them and remind them of the need for silence and secrecy.

'Martin Luther warns us that it will be dangerous,' she whispered, 'but he has been in contact with a sympathiser who will help, a man we can trust: Leonhard Koppe, a worthy burgher of Torgan.' They crowded round expectantly. 'This is the plan. Tomorrow night, Leonhard Koppe will draw up below this very window, with a large country cart loaded with an assortment of barrels – nine of them empty! We will have to climb down out of this window onto the cart and into the empty barrels.'

This information was greeted with gasps of horror all round the little cell. Katrina understood only too well, for she too had been horrified when she first read the plan of action, but having had time to reflect and consider the alternatives, she knew that it was a risk they had to take. Leonhard Koppe reckoned it would take about three days for them to reach Wittenberg. The thought of going to Wittenberg cheered them up considerably – that was Luther's centre and once there they knew they would be safe. Katrina further reassured them that Martin Luther had promised that he would be responsi-

ble for their safety once they arrived. However, she had a
further warning to deliver to them – the route to Wittenberg
meant they would have to pass through some of the territory
ruled by Duke George of Saxony, an area which they all knew
was very hostile to Luther and his followers.

Katrina had no further need to call for silence because they
were all dumbstruck with fright as they considered the awful
possibilities of what could happen to them should they be discovered en route in George's Dukedom. Their pale faces had
suddenly turned deathly white. Katrina waited for all this to
sink in before reminding them that if it was risky for them,
how much more so for brave Leonhard Koppe? If he was
willing to take his life in his hands to help them escape, surely
they could trust him (with God's help) to get them safely to
Wittenberg? Katrina saw the anxiety of her friends, their
white knuckles betraying the depths of their inner fears. She
waited and prayed silently, trying to hide her terror, for she
knew she had to allow them to make up their own minds. She
could not – would not – pressurise them.

Eventually, first one, then another, and another, nodded
brave approval of the plan, until all of the young ladies had
expressed their agreement. Under Katrina's leadership the
final details of the plan were put before the group. One careless word could endanger them all. They could only take the
smallest number of things with them, which brought a wan
smile to their anxious faces, as in the convent their earthly
possessions were minimal. Any food – especially bread –
would be welcome. After prayer they parted even more
silently than when they had gathered: tomorrow night they
would be leaving the convent, all being well!

The following day seemed to drag on for ever, but night
finally fell and each one checked more than once that they had
got everything they needed. None of them changed their minds
and right on time they were all there in Katrina's cell, looking
and waiting for Leonhard Koppe's cart to roll to its appointed

place. He too was on time, and one by one they clambered down out of the window and into the waiting beer barrels. As they felt exposed standing on the cart they needed no urging to get in. Even the moment most of them had dreaded – when Leonhard Koppe put the lids on their barrels – was not as frightening as they had imagined throughout the day. In fact, it seemed to give them a sense of security. Now confined, they snuggled down into the sturdy embraces of their barrel-homes.

After what seemed an age the cart moved off, with a lurch that shook the barrels. The occupants breathed a heartfelt silent prayer of thanks that the journey to freedom was under way at last. Surely it was the strangest and most precious cargo ever to leave a convent.

Never had three days and nights seemed so long. Leonhard Koppe took advantage of deserted parts of the road to pull aside for welcome breaks, but the risks were great and he had to keep them to the minimum. Safety, not comfort, was the watchword. The young ladies were relieved when night fell again and they could stretch their cramped and aching limbs. They knew that their escape must have been discovered by now and that orders would have been issued to apprehend them if at all possible. Once safely through Duke George's territory they could breathe more freely, but every time they passed through a town or village and heard voices they were petrified lest they be discovered. The journey seemed interminable but at long last they heard the crack of Leonhard Koppe's whip and sensed that they were moving much faster. Suddenly the cart came to a halt, but their fears turned to prayerful thanks when they heard him shout, 'Right, ladies, we've arrived in Wittenberg and are among friends. You can come out now – you are safe.'

What a sight as all nine lids popped open and up stood the young nuns, blinking as the bright daylight hit them. And what a welcome they received from the good folks of Wittenberg, who clapped and cheered them and stretched out willing hands to help the brave young women down from the cart. Then the crowd parted to make way for the man they were all so eager to meet and thank, Martin Luther. He gave them the warmest of welcomes, followed by his assurance that all of them would be cared for by Wittenberg families who had opened their homes to them.

Katrina found that her new home was to be with the town clerk, Dr Reichenbach, and his family. Her companions were likewise introduced to their hosts, who wrinkled noses at the mixed aromas of strong German beer, salted fish, and so on that hung like a cloud over the nine nuns. This quickly turned to raucous laughter as it was suggested that maybe they should try living in a barrel for three days and see how fragrant they would be! It took more than one bath and more than one wash of their clothes before they were free of their unwanted 'perfumes'.

News of the convent escape quickly spread across Germany. It created heated discussions and was angrily condemned by many. When it became known that Martin Luther was the one responsible, his many enemies heated the situation to boiling point. But they got more than they bargained for when Luther sat down and penned a pamphlet in which he gave the story of a poor girl called Florentina who had been put in a convent at six years of age and made to take the veil when only eleven years old. At the age of fourteen she felt she had no vocation to be a nun but the abbess made it clear to her that she was a nun for life and had to make the best of it. Florentina, like Katrina, had written to Luther, but Florentina's letter was intercepted and she was given severe penances. Next she tried to communicate with her relations, but when this was discovered she was beaten, chained by the foot, and condemned to lifelong incarceration in a cell. However, she finally managed to escape and when her story was known, Luther published it so that people would realise what 'cloistery' was like, and he said he could tell of many similar cases.

In fact, Katrina's case was much the same. She had been

sent to the convent by her family when she was only ten years old. Her family was noble but impoverished and this was one way to get a daughter off their hands. Katrina had taken the veil at sixteen years of age. The sad truth was that this kind of thing had become accepted as a family arrangement over the generations by many noble German households.

The nine nuns quickly settled down to life in Wittenberg, and before long eight of them had received and accepted proposals of marriage. Katrina was no exception. She was of dignified appearance, with a high, fair forehead and bright eyes. A woman of much spirit and a great deal of ability, she was quickly noticed and appreciated. Indeed, when King Christian of Denmark paid a visit to Wittenberg, she attracted his notice and appreciation by her dignified demeanour.

It was not long before Katrina received a proposal and became engaged, but she soon realised her mistake and ended the engagement. Two other husbands were suggested to her but she was not interested. The truth was that Katrina found herself greatly attracted to Luther, and Luther could not help but notice this outstanding young woman, although at first he thought her proud and was rather afraid of her. It was impossible for Katrina to live in Wittenberg without constantly hearing stories of the greatness and courage of this man of God, and the more she heard the more impressed she became.

His preaching enlightened her as it had done many before her. His penetrating eyes and lively imagination fascinated her. Here in Wittenberg he was the professor of the university that had been established by Frederic, the Elector of Saxony, and Katrina soon began to realise the true greatness of Dr Martin Luther. He was a man of much learning who had given himself to master the word of God, and to do that thoroughly he had devoted himself to the study of Hebrew and Greek. But for all his learning, his preaching was easy to understand. He was a great communicator who made the Bible live – it was so different to anything she had ever heard.

Although she had been desperate to leave the convent her devotion to the Christian faith remained strong and, under the preaching and teaching of Luther, so much that previously had been a mystery became clear to her.

Soon something else became obvious to her as well: Luther was overworked and took little care of himself. It was common knowledge that in his early days as an Augustinian monk he had practised asceticism to dangerous extremes. He fasted, prayed and abused his body with scourgings and want of sleep. At least once he went three full days without food or water. Missing from a service on one occasion he was later discovered unconscious on the floor of his cell. Naturally such practices took their toll of his health.

Luther was first called to the recently founded university at Wittenberg in 1508, but the founder (Frederic the Elector of Saxony) was short of funds. Luther had already distinguished himself as an outstanding scholar, but the appointment of monks as professors in theology and philosophy owed just as much to the fact that monks would not be paid a salary. As a consequence he was always short of funds, which meant that his diet was frequently inadequate.

Katrina continued to glean scraps of information about her hero. It was all too obvious that he was seriously neglecting himself. With a little help from three of her companions, who for a time had been helping with domestic duties in the old friary, she learned that Luther's bed had not been changed in a year!

The serious and growing unrest among the German peasants, coupled with outbreaks of the deadly plague, had disrupted life everywhere. Wittenberg, the key centre with Luther as the accepted leader of the rising Reformation, was affected more than most places. The pressures upon him were tremendous – he was too busy to eat properly, snatching hurried meals, until by the end of the day he was so tired he just fell into his sweaty, unmade bed. Inevitably his health suffered: he had ringing in his ears, and the first signs of gallstones. He had abandoned his monastic garb for the usual dress of a German professor and his enemies sneeringly accused him of 'living a soft life at Wittenberg'. Whereas, in truth, for several years at least, he was rattling around in the old friary, deserted by all the monks except himself and one other (Prior Brisger) with no servant to look after them.

Luther, who was working himself almost to death, was often reduced to dining on bread and water. He needed someone to look after him. Katrina pondered deep and long – was this to be her new vocation in life? Was marriage out of the question? If it were possible . . . permissible even . . . she would love to do it; but was it? She prayed about it, feeling a sense of urgency for two good reasons: Luther's health was clearly deteriorating, and her age was increasing. Although she was only approaching her mid-twenties, most men regarded that as too old for marriage – as her erstwhile suitors and companions were quick to remind her.

Luther made no secret of the fact that he had long been convinced that there was no reason why parish priests should practise celibacy if they preferred a married life. He believed that men and women who had been forced to take monastic vows in early years, without a definite sense of a calling, were at liberty to leave their cloisters. However, he was not persuaded that men like himself, who had embraced the monastic life solely on their own decision, were in a similar position when it came to celibacy. Even after he reached the conclusion that those vows were based on a warped idea of true righteousness, and so misleading that they were, in truth, invalid, he was not inclined to consider marriage for himself.

But his teaching on marriage lifted it out of the extremely low view that then prevailed. It had become generally accepted that the union between husband and wife was comparatively unholy and even sullied the lives of Christians who shared in it. This teaching was accepted almost without question, in spite of the fact that the Scriptures hallowed marriage by comparing it with the union between Christ and his church, not to mention other texts that declared in clearest terms, 'Marriage should be honoured by all, and the marriage bed kept pure . . .' (Hebrews 13:4). A large percentage of medieval parish priests, while finding celibacy too great a strain, refused to marry, but resorted to concubinage, until the practice became almost universal.

The times were already dangerous and difficult, which was one reason why the university in Wittenberg was almost bereft of students, and faculty apart from Luther. The dawn of 1525 found Luther's good friend, the Elector, very ill and with little hope of recovery, and the country was in the throes of what was fast becoming a full-scale civil war. The peasants, driven by their extreme poverty, were now in open revolt and robbing and murdering. Luther's health was deteriorating and the turmoil the country was in meant that there was the possibility that law officers might seize the opportunity to descend upon Wittenberg and carry Luther off. The result of that could be death and so it was that Luther rejected any thought of marriage.

By springtime the violence grew worse, and with the Elector's health deteriorating still further, the outlook was not good. However, Luther managed to squeeze in a visit to his parents. His sturdy old father – against the prevailing opinion of the age – held high views of marriage and home life, and he made no secret of the fact that he was still longing for grandchildren from Martin.

By the time he returned to Wittenberg Luther had finally made up his mind about marrying. The decision was his own, so much so that he had already decided that he would not seek advice on the matter from even his closest and oldest friends. He did not want anyone trying either to persuade or dissuade him. There was, of course, one other rather important matter still to be decided – a bride!

Luther, with typical bluntness, would never disclose details about his proposal. He said repeatedly over the years that such matters ought to be left in the hands of God and the two persons concerned. All we know for sure is that soon after his return to Wittenberg he sought out Katrina and asked her to marry him. From the time of her arrival in the barrel, Katrina felt in her heart that Martin Luther was the man for her; and somewhere along the line, he decided that Katrina had all the requirements to make him a true wife.

The date was fixed for 13th June 1525. Having at last reached this momentous decision – and it was a tremendous step for the two of them to take, a former monk marrying an ex-nun – it was also another vital demonstration of their full commitment to all that the Reformation meant to them. On the evening of that extraordinary day, in the simplest of services in the old friary with the parish priest and a handful of friends, the common German ceremony of marriage was gone through before the witnesses. The couple were asked whether they would take one another for man and wife; they were then directed to take each other by the right hand, and were declared to be 'joined together in holy matrimony, in the name of the Triune God'.

Luther had ceased to accept that marriage was a true church sacrament to be placed alongside communion and baptism, and no wedding ceremony in church was necessary as far as he was concerned. A few days later the married couple gave a modest breakfast to their more intimate friends. Two weeks later on 27th June the wedding was celebrated at a feast, to which relations, including his father and mother, and friends were invited. Among the guests was Leonhard Koppe, whose cart and barrels had made it all possible.

Luther was approaching forty-two years of age and Katrina was twenty-six. The new elector gave them the old Augustinian friary for a house and in spite of the fact that there had been no courtship, the two of them were soon enjoying married life to the full. It was an excellent marriage for both of them and although before marriage Luther had said that there had been no emotional or sexual fascination, he was soon enjoying Katrina's presence 'in both bed and house'.

Their first year of married life was extremely happy. Luther soon discovered what a treasure of a wife God had given him. She was an outstanding woman with many gifts and talents and it did not take her long to transform their living conditions. His affection and growing esteem for her are reflected in the way he addressed her. Henceforth it was Katie rather than Katrina. When he was away from home his letters revealed his loving heart, his high regard for her, and his humour. He addressed her as 'My Lord Katie' – making it obvious who was running the home! Then, because she was an early riser, as 'My Morning Star'. He loved to have her with him whenever possible; he even liked to have her sit with him in his study. Very soon they were both companion and friend to each other. Katie took charge of their domestic life and in many ways she 'managed' Luther extremely well in areas where he clearly needed it. But she was very tolerant of his reactions which, on occasion, were guaranteed to raise more than a few eyebrows. On occasions he was quite coarse though never obscene. He also took delight in deliberately provoking Katie just to hear her spirited response, which often took him by surprise because her command of the German language was as good – if not better – as his own, and his was outstanding.

Within a few months Luther's happiness reached even greater heights when Katie told him she was pregnant. Their first child, a son, was born on 8th June 1526, almost exactly a year after their wedding. They named him Johann. Although they were still very poor (Luther had next to nothing when they married, and Katie literally had nothing as a former nun now disowned by her family), as a new, proud father he was elated. He wrote to a friend, 'I would not exchange my poverty for the riches of Croesus.' His happy humour was irrepressible and to another trusted friend he finished his letter, 'My Rib and I send greetings to you and your rib' –

referring of course to God creating Eve from Adam's rib. Luther's life was transformed. He was now experiencing what he had believed was the sort of home and relationship every Christian family should have, that is, 'family life lit by the faith of the Gospel . . . which made the family fireside as sacred as a monastic cell, and a mother's vigil over a sick child as holy as a nun's on the flags of a convent'.[1]

The second year of married life presented them with difficulties that tested their love to the limits. Martin became desperately ill in 1527. Katie, in spite of being pregnant again and experiencing severe nausea, nursed him with loving skill, and he was cheered by the smiles of his little son. But Martin was saddened at the possibility of dying and leaving Johann fatherless and Katie a widow without any means of support. Katie bravely faced up to the frightening prospect of losing her beloved husband and told him, '. . . if it be God's will then I also choose that you be with Him rather than with me. It is not so much I and my child that need you as the multitude of pious Christian people. Take no thought of me.' Her courage lifted him and her tender nursing brought him back from the brink of death.

Just when it seemed there was hope of things returning to some semblance of normality, the dreaded plague hit Wittenberg. The university and Court left town and the Elector pleaded with Martin to follow. He refused, declaring that he would not play the hireling and flee when the sheep needed him most. Within a matter of days there were eighteen victims who had succumbed to the plague, including some of their closest friends. In the midst of all this chaos, Katie gave birth to a daughter, Elizabeth, and her cool courage was an example and inspiration to everyone. Then Johann fell ill. At first it was feared that it was the plague, but fortunately it was not and in due time, to their great relief, he recovered.

---

[1] John M. Todd, *Luther – A Life* (Hamish Hamilton 1982), p. 202.

Rising hopes were once again dashed when news reached them that a faithful Bavarian pastor had been burnt at the stake. The greatness and true worth of Luther was revealed in his reaction to all this by his sitting down and composing his stirring, world-famous hymn:

> A safe stronghold our God is still,
>  A trusty shield and weapon;
> He'll help us clear from all the ill
>  That hath us now o'ertaken.

At long last the plague ended and the students and professors returned to Wittenberg. With his old friends around him and the domestic skills of Katie transforming their accommodation, Luther's health and his spirits were restored. With Katie by his side he was his old self once again – and even more. With womanly intuition she set about creating new interests for him to help counter the tremendous load of work he carried. She set to work on the neglected garden so that it soon took on a different air, and before long she had Martin sitting in the garden with her, relaxing. She persuaded him to write to friends for seeds and plants, and his life – though still busy – took on an altogether more balanced and beautiful aspect. It was not long before he was not only writing for seeds, but with Katie's tactful suggestions was planting them as well.

He loved lecturing in the university, which was beginning to bustle with life and energy once more. Their large dwelling enabled Katie to keep open doors of hospitality for students as well as their own 'extended and ever extending family'. Katie continued to bear children and they eventually had three sons and two daughters. Her aunt, Magdalena von Bora, who was in the convent when Katie joined, finally followed in Katie's steps and left her life as a nun for life at Wittenberg with Martin and Katie and their family. Other relatives also swelled the family circle, as well as a number of students who boarded with them.

Life was never dull or quiet. Over the years Luther's *Table Talk* was written and published. The evening meal was nearly always followed with music and singing, and he especially loved having his children sing to him. His humour frequently surfaced and the laughter often became raucous. Some thought his humour went too far, but Katie was wisely tolerant, knowing only too well that with the load of responsibility he carried and the expectations that people had of him, he needed such times to relieve the pressures which, although changing, were still enormous.

Without Katie to look after him, it is the considered opinion of many that he would not have survived more than two and a half years after their marriage. Instead, they enjoyed twenty-one very wonderful years of married life.

Katie was constantly discovering the many talents of her increasingly famous husband, whose name had become known throughout the whole of Europe. She realised that one reason why he was such a formidable debater was that in his early days as a student at university he had studied logic. Martin for his part never ceased to be amazed at Katie's range of skills and interests. She was a marvellous mother and a faithful wife who made sure that life ran smoothly and efficiently. Not content with making the garden beautiful and profitable, she turned her attention to farming in a small way with pigs and poultry. Such ventures were necessary during the first years of their marriage when Martin's income was pitifully inadequate. It was not until 1532 that his professorial salary was raised to a more acceptable level. Katie was invaluable to him; she assisted him with his correspondence and her more diplomatic approach helped considerably. She was one of his trusted inner circle who sought to guide and direct the growing tide of the Reformation.

The death of baby Elizabeth in 1528 hit them both hard. The sad experience reveals how marriage and fatherhood had softened him. Martin confessed he was surprised at the greatness of his grief as a father at the loss of their precious daughter who had brought such happiness to them. He wrote to a friend, 'Never before would I have believed that a father's heart could have such tender feelings to his child.'

Luther's achievements were many, but one of his greatest and most lasting was the production of the German Bible. His love affair with the word of God dates back to his early days in the monastery and at university. As soon as he had free access to a complete Bible in Latin (Jerome's famous translation, known as the Vulgate) Luther was captivated. He read it and read it, even before the wonderful day of his enlightenment. That came only after long, pain-filled years of seeking and searching for the truth. At last, the gospel of God's saving grace shone into his heart from the text 'The just shall live by faith.' In his own words:

> Before those words broke upon my mind, I hated God and was angry with him because not content with frightening us sinners by the law and by the miseries of life, he still further increased our torture by the gospel. But when, by the Spirit of God, I understood these words – 'The just shall live by faith', then I felt born again like a new man; I entered through the open doors into the very paradise of God. Henceforward I saw the beloved and Holy Scriptures with other eyes. The words that I had previously detested, I began from that hour to value and love as the sweetest and most consoling words in the Bible.[2]

Luther's burning desire was to share the Good News of God's saving grace in Christ and through his cross, and he did his utmost to ensure that his preaching was simple enough for the most uneducated peasant to understand. (Although, when called by the emperor to give account at the Diet of Worms in 1521, for example, he was capable of the most eloquent and unanswerable logic and rhetoric.) Therefore when he undertook the formidable task of translating the Bible into

---

[2] A. Skevington Wood, *Captive to the Word* (Paternoster 1969), pp. 51–52.

German, his overwhelming passion was to produce a faithful and accurate translation in the everyday language of the people. He worked on it for years with a small, select group of scholars. The New Testament was published and printed in 1522, but translating the Old Testament was a greater task, not completed until 1534. The greatness of this work is seen by the fact that his translation of the Bible remained good for some four hundred years, earning praise from Catholic and Protestant alike.

Martin needed Katie perhaps even more than ever. His health was still poor, but he survived and continued to cope with a massive workload, thanks largely to her domestic skills and wifely care. And how he needed her, for in 1535 the plague struck again. Once again most of the members of the university moved away to safer areas, but not Martin and Katie. In his letters he reveals how proud he was of Katie: 'The chief cook, our Lord Katie . . . sends greetings . . . she drives the wagon, takes care of the fields, buys and puts cattle out to pasture, brews good beer. . . .' But she was spiritual as well as practical and Martin goes on to say, 'In between she starts to read the Bible, and I have promised her fifty guilden if she finishes before Easter . . . she is very serious.' His devotion to her comes out again and again in such 'asides' as the following:

> . . . the husband confides all his secrets to his wife. . . . I would not part from Katie for all France and Venice. . . . Next to God's Word, the world has no more precious treasure than a holy matrimony. . . . God's best gift is a pious, cheerful, God-fearing, home-keeping wife, with whom you may live peacefully, to whom you may entrust your goods, your body, your life.[3]

His *Table Talk* reveals that there were no 'his' and 'hers' towels in their home, for, he said, 'Between husband and wife

---

[3] T. M. Lindsay, *Luther and the German Reformation* (T. & T. Clark 1900), p. 202.

there is no question of meum and teum [mine and thine]; they have all things in common between them.'

Katie made sure the home was a haven from all the turmoil outside. Their family life was loving and happy. Music regularly featured after the evening meal when he loved to have his children sing to him – he even wrote a carol specially for them. On one occasion when Martin was forced to be away for quite a long period at Coburg, Katie on learning via his secretary that he was missing them terribly, got their good friend Lucas Cranach, an artist, to paint a portrait of their one-year-old baby Magdalena. When Martin received the picture he hung it up where he could always see it and it achieved the results Katie had been praying for: it gave him fresh courage and cheered him through three more long months of waiting.

When at last he was free to return to them in Wittenberg his cup of happiness overflowed. But life continued to be one of incessant labours and deteriorating health; twice he was at death's door, and yet again he thwarted death. However, in January 1546 he was forced to travel to Eisleben. The weather was atrocious and the rivers in flood, prolonging the journey and adding to his woes. By mid-February the business he had been attending to was at last settled and he wrote to 'My dear kind housewife, Katie Luther von Bora, at Wittenberg', telling her that all was well and that he hoped to be home within the week. He preached in the Church of St Andrew at Eisleben on 14th February (the same day that he wrote his letter to her), and he preached with great power and fervour, but four days later he became very ill and died in the early hours of Thursday, 18th February.

Katie's happiness at the thoughts of Martin's homecoming was turned to deepest sadness when the news reached her of his sudden death and that his homecoming would now be his final one. Two months afterwards, Katie wrote to her sister, 'Who would not be sorrowful and mourn for so noble a man? Truly I am so distressed I cannot tell the deep sorrow in my heart to anybody. . . . If I had an empire it would never have cost me so much pain to lose it as I have now that our Lord God has taken from me this dear and precious man. . . .'

So ended this beautiful love affair between the monk and the nun, but through their love for each other and for the Son of God and the word of God, they bequeathed a legacy of light and true love that is still blessing the world after the passing of half a millennium. A letter in the handwriting of their youngest son, Paul, reads:

> In the year 1544 my late dearest father, in the presence of us all, narrated the whole story of his journey to Rome. He acknowledged with great joy, that in that city, through the Spirit of Jesus Christ, he had come to the knowledge of the truth of the everlasting gospel. It happened in this way. As he repeated his prayers on the Lateran staircase the words of the Prophet Habakkuk came suddenly to his mind, 'The just shall live by faith.' Thereupon he ceased his prayers, returned to Wittenberg, and took this as the chief foundation of all his doctrine.[4]

On another occasion Martin Luther said, 'In very truth, this text was to me the true gate of Paradise. An open door into the very Paradise of God.' That was the secret of his life, the secret he shared with Katie, the secret behind their happy marriage, and an open secret for all to share today.

The epistle of Galatians, with the apostle Paul's inspired exposition of Habakkuk's text 'The just shall live by faith', was a favourite of Martin Luther. His love of it and his love for Katie are beautifully expressed in some words he wrote, 'Galatians was my own little epistle. I have betrothed myself to it, it is my Katie von Bora.'

---

[4]  F. W. Boreham, *A Bunch of Everlastings* (Abingdon Press 1920).

# 2

## *Charles and Sarah Wesley*

Sarah Gwynne gazed into the splendid mirror adorning her elegant dressing table and sighed a gentle sigh. Everyone, including her personal maid, told her she was very pretty – but as she examined her young face in the mirror (she was under twenty years of age) she was not fully persuaded. And even if they were right, was an attractive face the most important thing in life? Certainly some of her friends were much prettier than her, but several of them were also rather empty-headed.

Sarah took after her father in many ways. Like him, she treated religion seriously, thought about God and pondered about the real meaning and purpose of life. As she was rich her clothes were beautiful and, according to her mother, 'she was one of the most fortunate young ladies in the whole of South Wales'. That was easier to accept, not just because her mother told her so several times a week, but because Garth House, their home overlooking the winding river, was splendid and she loved it.

Her father was the Squire of Garth, near Builth Wells; he was also a magistrate and a devout churchman. She had eight brothers and sisters, some of whom were already married into other leading families and prospering, thanks largely to her

mother, who was more money conscious than her father. Life
at Garth House was well run with twenty servants, and there
were many interesting house guests – sometimes a dozen or
more.

Her reverie in front of the mirror was cut short by the
sounding of the breakfast gong. She hurried downstairs, well
aware of Mother's insistence on promptness. Sarah was surprised on entering the dining room to find her father already
taking his leave of her mother who was obviously displeased
about something. She quickly learned the reason: her father
had a warrant to arrest a young Welsh preacher by the name
of Howell Harris, whose fiery preaching seemed to be causing
riots all around the area. A schoolteacher, Harris was not an
ordained clergyman and in the eyes of many (including
Sarah's mother) that meant his preaching was 'irregular'. For
Mrs Gwynne this was reason enough for her husband to
arrange to have him arrested. But the squire insisted that first,
in all fairness, he must go and hear the man and judge for
himself.

Sarah's sympathies were with her father. She felt closer to
him, even though she had the honour of bearing the same
Christian name as her mother, whose maiden name was Sarah
Evans. The Evans family were very rich and each one of their
six daughters inherited £30,000, a considerable fortune in
those days. However, her father, Marmaduke Gwynne, was
even richer – but there was a shadow over the Gwynne
family's past. His grandfather, also named Marmaduke, had
been a barrister who had married a London heiress and had
succeeded in being appointed a judge in North Wales. Alas,
he was removed from that high office on charges of corrup-
tion, but not before he had managed to acquire the manor of
Garth as well as most of Builth. Sarah's father was high-
principled and intent on living down the past. After graduating from Jesus College, Oxford, he had entered Lincoln's Inn
and was eventually appointed Sheriff of Radnorshire. Sarah

admired her father for his integrity and understood why he insisted on making his own judgement about Howell Harris. She was impatient for him to return so that she could find out what had happened.

However, even Sarah was taken aback at the turn of events when Marmaduke returned home that evening. Mrs Gwynne greeted him and immediately wanted to know all about his arrest of the upstart preacher. When Marmaduke informed her that, far from arresting young Harris he was so impressed with him that he had brought him home to meet the family, she could not believe that he could do such a thing. Refusing point-blank to meet him, she left the scene in tears. Sarah, on the other hand, was eager to meet him. Mrs Gwynne's tears and shock were far from over; she was left speechless (a rare event indeed) when next she learned that Marmaduke and Sarah were attending Howell Harris's services on a regular basis. The news, which followed shortly afterwards – that Marmaduke Gwynne, the Squire of Garth, Magistrate and Sheriff, was not only attending Harris's services, along with his daughter Sarah, but had been converted – caused a sensation across the whole area. Eager gossips passed the news: 'The squire's got converted.' Its effect upon Mrs Gwynne was to leave her staggered beyond belief.

Marmaduke, however, was no fool and his lawyer's instincts ensured that he would have a good case to defend, especially before that most formidable critic, his good wife. So he made sure he knew everything possible about Howell Harris and his friends, the leaders of the growing Methodist Movement, the Revds John and Charles Wesley. The fact that the Wesleys were Oxford graduates, as he was, impressed him – and also Mrs Gwynne, whose opposition was slowly crumbling. Even so, she also made it her business to ask around about Howell Harris and the Wesley brothers and found, to her surprise and relief, that the Wesleys were held in high esteem by those of her acquaintances who had studied at

Oxford. Her lingering reservations were finally overcome by John Wesley's new book *Appeal to Men of Reason and Religion*. His logical and scriptural presentation of his case convinced her and it was not long before she was welcoming Methodist preachers to Garth House. Marmaduke made it his business to attend the Wesleys' 1745 conference in Bristol where he was further strengthened in his new-found faith and in his confidence in the Methodist Movement. He was able to see for himself the amazing changes the Methodist Revival had made at Kingswood, some four miles from the centre of Bristol.

When Marmaduke returned home he could not wait to share the thrilling story with his wife and the ever-eager Sarah. They listened open-mouthed as he described it all to them. Before the Methodist Revival the Kingswood coal miners had the reputation of being probably the most depraved people in Britain. They worked stark naked, and were notorious for drunkenness, violence, wife beating and degradation of every kind, including sodomy.

George Whitefield (a former member of the Holy Club when at Oxford) was the first to preach to the Kingswood miners, with hundreds turning to Christ in the most dramatic fashion, and with lasting results. In 1739 Whitefield left for America again but not before persuading John Wesley to help and care for the Kingswood work during his absence. It was the first time John had preached in the fields and marked the beginning of his open-air preaching, which God confirmed with similar demonstrations of power.

Charles paid his first visit to Bristol the following year and was there for two memorable months. (The foundation stone of the first Methodist building – known as the New Room – had been laid on 12th May 1739.) Charles was another who could not wait to witness the mighty happenings at Kingswood and within two days of arriving he was among the colliers, squatters and roving thieves, ministering to them with great power. Charles soon found himself preaching to crowds of five thousand and more in the open air. People of all kinds, educated and ignorant, rich and poor, were brought to saving faith in Christ. There was opposition and persecution as well, but Charles found Bristol to his liking. Then the second largest city in Britain, it was destined to become a Methodist stronghold.

Mrs Gwynne and Sarah wanted to hear Marmaduke's impressions of the Wesley brothers after attending the Bristol conference. He left his wife and daughter in no doubt that he thought them two of the most remarkable men it had been his privilege to meet. They were certainly not fanatics, but learned, balanced, humble servants of Christ with a consuming passion to make their Saviour known to all. One of John's memorable sayings was, 'The world is my parish.'

A month later, Marmaduke heard that Charles Wesley was staying at Fonmon Castle, near Barry, with the young squire, Robert Jones, also a convert of Howell Harris and an Oxford contemporary of Charles. He immediately despatched a servant with an invitation for Charles to return with their man and be their guest at Garth House. They were all disappointed, however (none more so than Sarah), when the servant returned alone bearing the sad news that Charles was unable to accept their kind invitation: he was laid up with a leg injury, and although he had been preaching while on crutches, he was not well enough to undertake the journey. So eager were the Gwynnes for Charles to visit them, that a week later Marmaduke travelled to Fonmon Castle to renew the invitation in person; but Charles was still unable to accept.

Sarah had to possess her soul in patience for two more years before meeting Charles. However, she and her mother and father prayed for him and sought for every scrap of news about him on his constant travels. They were deeply moved as Marmaduke shared some of the anecdotes he had picked up at the Bristol conference relating to Charles's prison ministry, especially those about London's notorious Newgate Prison where, on one occasion, an antagonistic jailor maliciously locked Charles in the prison yard. There, completely unruffled, Charles climbed onto a bench and started preaching to the prisoners who clambered to their cell windows to listen. In the end the jailor was glad to let him out and Charles was sad to have to leave! The stories about his ministry to condemned prisoners reduced them to tears and Sarah made a mental note to be sure to get the stories first-hand from Charles himself . . . but when would that be? Did he ever get off his horse long enough to chat?

The more Sarah heard about Charles, the more her young heart was captivated by him, even though they had not met. Meanwhile, she had to content herself with collecting all the information about him that she could. Bit by bit she built up a fuller picture of this intriguing, and 'annoying', man who seemed to be able to visit everywhere except Garth House!

Sarah had no difficulty in putting together a picture of Charles's early years. She discovered that he was born on 18th December 1707 in the Epworth rectory in North Lincolnshire, where his father, Revd Samuel Wesley, was the vicar. His mother, Susanna, the youngest daughter of Dr Samuel Annesley, was well educated, capable and good looking. Both parents could trace their family connections back to the peerage. Sarah gasped when she uncovered the story of a fire at the Epworth rectory in 1709 from which Charles's older brother, John, had been rescued just in the nick of time before the roof collapsed. Baby Charles (then about 18 months old) had been grabbed by the maid when the alarm was raised, and carried to safety. More surprises followed when she learned that arson was suspected.

She was amazed to discover that Susanna had nineteen children, of whom only six survived, including sons Samuel, John and Charles. The youngest boy, and eighteenth child, was premature and so weak at birth that it was two months before he cried or opened his eyes. In spite of producing a baby every year, the remarkable Susanna (who knew Greek and Latin) succeeded in teaching all of her children. She was firm and rather severe with them: after being disciplined they were also taught to 'cry softly'!

Samuel, John and Charles went on to excel academically and, when he was nine years old, Charles followed in the steps of his oldest brother, Samuel, and was sent to Westminster School – one of the best and most famous schools in the land. Samuel had already progressed to becoming a teacher there and generously assumed financial responsibility for Charles's education. This was necessary because their parents were poor and constantly in debt (Revd Samuel Wesley, Senior, was once hauled off to Lincoln Prison for being in debt).

For the first five years at Westminster School, Charles lodged with his brother Samuel. He succeeded in becoming a King's Scholar at fourteen years of age, which meant his education was free and he could move into the dormitory for King's Scholars. A good mixer and popular, he indulged in the usual schoolboy pranks – including a few fights on the Green. It was said that in this he was following after his father who had a reputation for being impulsive and rather hot-tempered. Charles, no coward, once jumped to the defence of a new boy (James Murray) who was being subjected to ridicule because of his Scottish accent and for being a Jacobite. This act of courageous kindness was never forgotten by the boy, who remained a friend even when he became Lord Mansfield, Lord Chief Justice of England. All the boys had to speak Latin throughout the school day as well as study Greek, and Charles became a fine classical scholar. In his final year he was honoured by being made head boy and by gaining a studentship at Christ Church, Oxford, after coming top of the Westminster candidates. However, on his own admission, he wasted most of his first year at Oxford by indulging in the many 'diversions' that university life presented – though his lack of funds did not provide him with much scope.

In his second year, after a brotherly warning from John, he took steps to rectify matters and in 1727 formed the Holy Club, the purpose of which was to gather a small number of like-minded students in an informal group for the better use of their time in methodical study and prayer. They also began some social work among the poor and did some prison visiting. They earned themselves many nicknames, including 'Bible moths', and the one Sarah had often wondered about as to its origin, 'Methodists'. After graduating and becoming a tutor, Charles and the Holy Club continued in Oxford.

In 1735 Charles (having been persuaded to be ordained) left Oxford along with John to go out to the new colony of Georgia in America, John as Pastor to the first settlers in Savannah, Charles as Secretary to the Governor, General Oglethorpe. The voyage out on the *Simmonds* was stormy and characterised the whole of their American adventure, which was nearly a fiasco from beginning to end. Charles was both homesick and physically sick, and within fourteen months was back in England (the voyage home was equally dangerous, due more to the drunken captain than to the dangers of the ocean).

Back home in England Charles was still not well physically but travelled around a good deal, only to find that travelling on land in England was almost as dangerous as in Georgia, after he was held up and robbed by an armed highwayman. His voyage across the Atlantic to Georgia had made him something of a celebrity, such journeys still being undertaken by only a few people. The Archbishop of Canterbury nominated Charles to present an address on behalf of the University of Oxford to the King at Hampton Court and the following day he dined with the Prince of Wales at St James's Palace. But Charles, like John, was still seeking God for a clearer understanding of the gospel. John was not long after Charles in returning to England, likewise disillusioned and disappointed; he wrote in his journal, on 24th January 1738, 'I went to America, to convert the Indians; but, O! who shall convert me?' Their quest for the truth of the gospel of Christ was nearing its end, and in retrospect they would be able to see the over-ruling hand of God in everything – even their unhappy days in America.

Sarah continued to gather information about Charles and found it hard to believe the amount of travelling he put in, month after month, year after year. Just what was it that kept two Oxford academics galloping on horseback around England, Scotland, Ireland and Wales, in all kinds of weather, visiting prisons, preaching Christ to condemned criminals, and constantly braving attacks by angry mobs brandishing clubs and throwing stones? She longed to ask Charles the reason why.

In 1747 her patience was at last rewarded. Charles, on his way to Ireland, broke his journey at Maemynis to stay with his friend Revd Edward Phillips, where he had also arranged to meet John, who was returning from Ireland. As soon as the Gwynne family heard that Charles was there, Marmaduke called on him and renewed his invitation to Garth House. Charles accepted but said that he was due to preach in Llandrindod the next day, after which he would most gladly come to them.

Charles warmed to the Gwynnes and was immediately at ease in their company; the feeling was mutual and they were all favourably impressed by him – especially Sarah, who found herself drawn to him. Short though the visit was, Sarah was determined not to let this fascinating man ride off to Holyhead for the Irish ferry before she had got him to tell them just how it had all started. They had heard garbled accounts of the Wesley brothers' conversions, but they wanted it straight from the horse's mouth, so to speak!

Charles was good company and easy to approach, and after the splendid meal, which Mrs Gwynne had planned in honour of his first visit to Garth House, they all settled into comfortable chairs around a crackling log fire to hear his own account of his conversion.

It was a story Charles was always ready to tell, especially to people who wanted to hear it; and everyone there certainly did. He glanced round at the eager faces, and stopped a moment longer as he came to Sarah, a charming young lady and obviously spiritually aware. Conscious of her bright young eyes fixed upon him, he launched into his story, and from the first word he had them riveted, for he knew how to tell a story as well as to preach. At Westminster School he had taken part in the school plays and loved acting. The telling of his story was embellished with numerous hand and arm actions, subtle changes of voice as he mimicked those involved, as well as delightful touches of humour that drew happy outbursts of laughter. They were all spellbound as he unfolded his story. But first he explained the book in his hand: his journal containing his own personal account, written at the time.

He described how on the journey out to Georgia he and his brother John had found that, in spite of being ordained clergymen, when brought face to face with death during the terrible storm that nearly wrecked the ship, the faith they had was not enough to overcome their fear of death. Their stay in Georgia had been a disappointment from start to finish, and the voyage home had been another nightmare. Shortly after returning to England he was taken ill in April 1738, and he explained how he had made the decision to leave the comfortable apartment he shared with a wealthy friend and colleague. He moved to the humble home of a Mr Bray, a lowly brazier by trade, who lived over his shop in Little Britain.

The reason for the decision, which had upset both his friend and his friend's mother (who had offered her luxurious home to him until his health was restored), was that Mr Bray had a deep experience and knowledge of Christ as Saviour and Lord, something none of Charles's friends had. Charles was so ill that he had to be carried in a chair from his friend's home to Mr Bray's, where a doctor diagnosed him as having pleurisy. In his weakness he prayed earnestly for God to help him. Mr Bray assisted him greatly, but in the end it was his sister, Mrs Turner, whom Mr Bray had led to Christ only a few days before, that God used as his instrument.

On the morning of Whit Sunday, 21st May, Charles awoke with hope in his heart (though still confined to his sickbed). He was cheered by a visit from his brother John and some friends, who, it being Pentecost Day, sang a hymn whose theme was for the Spirit of God to come to them as at that first Pentecost. After John and the friends had left, Charles prayed, 'O Jesus, Thou hast said, "I will come unto you," Thou hast said, "I will send the Comforter unto you."' He described that he was just settling down to sleep when he heard a woman's voice, which he thought he recognised, and which said with unusual strength, 'In the name of Jesus of Nazareth, arise, and believe, and thou shalt be healed.' The words struck Charles to the heart and he found himself wondering if it was Christ speaking to him. He rang the little handbell on his bedside table and Mrs Turner came in. She then left on the arrival of Mr Bray. After some earnest conversation with Mr Bray, Mrs Turner came back into the room and confessed that she was the one who had spoken those words: 'It was I, a weak, sinful creature, spoke; but the words were Christ's: He commanded me to say them, and so constrained me that I could not forbear.' Charles told Mr Bray that he did believe, and after a time of inner conflict, said that he found himself convinced.

The silence in the room could be felt. He had told the story in such a way that to the listeners it seemed as if they were there with him in his bedroom over the shop. But when he proceeded to tell them the rest of the story, their eyes opened even wider. Mr Bray told Charles how his sister had wanted to speak to him, but felt that it would have been presumptuous of her to speak to a clergyman in this way. In the end she felt she must. Around the same night that Charles was first taken ill, Mrs Turner had had a remarkable, vivid dream in which she heard a knock at the door. On opening it and seeing a person in white standing there she caught hold of him and asked who he was. She received the answer 'I am Jesus Christ.' Whereupon she cried out loudly, 'Come in! Come in!' and then awoke in a state of great fright. At the Friday evening prayer time she found herself so full of faith and power that she prayed as she had never been able to pray before – with freedom and a great love for all mankind, especially for Charles. She felt she had to go and assure him from Christ of his recovery, soul and body. After the evening prayers she returned home full of joy; but then, when it came to speaking to Charles, her courage failed her.

On Whit Sunday morning she told her brother (Mr Bray) what had happened and burst into tears when explaining how she felt she had to give Charles this message, but lacked the faith to do so. He prayed with her and encouraged her to be obedient and speak to Charles as directed.

Charles said that the result of all this was that at long last, after years of earnest seeking, he found himself at peace with God, and rejoicing in hope of loving Christ. Two days later he celebrated his conversion experience by writing a new hymn:

> Where shall my wond'ring soul begin?
> How shall I all to Heaven aspire?
> A slave redeemed from death and sin,
> A brand plucked from eternal fire?

Charles prayed for his brother John, and later, when they had checked their journals, he found that John had written, 'I received the surprising news that my brother had found rest to his soul. His bodily strength returned also from that hour.'

Three days later, on 24th May, John's journal described how he had 'unwillingly' attended a meeting in Aldersgate Street, and about a quarter to nine, 'I felt my heart strangely warmed. I felt I did trust in Christ, Christ alone, for salvation; and an assurance was given me that He had taken away my sins, even mine, and saved me from the law of sin and death.'

Charles closed his journal and looked around at his little group of entranced listeners. There was only one thing they could do: pray. Next day with great reluctance they watched Charles mount his horse and ride off to Holyhead for the Irish ferry to Dublin. Sarah's prayers – and her heart – went with him.

Sarah was impatient for news from Ireland; but when it came mother and daughter were deeply disturbed. On arriving in Dublin Charles had found the Methodist preaching house destroyed by a Catholic mob; his first task was to comfort the distressed members as he preached in the ruins of the building. Out on the streets he was pursued by violent crowds shouting insults, backed up with showers of stones. Despite the risks he preached on St Stephen's Green, aware that earlier in the day a constable had been beaten, killed and his body strung up for all to see – and no one had been arrested. The city was seething with unrest and his arrival only increased it, the old feuds between Catholics and Protestants as bitter as ever. The only thing that seemed to unite the two groups was their hatred of the Methodists! With great courage and fearless preaching eventually the Catholics listened to him.

This, his first visit to Ireland, lasted for six action-packed, dangerous months, during which he collected enough funds to buy land and build another chapel in Dublin. He travelled around Ireland with contrasting receptions; some people listened eagerly, others could not wait to attack him and his companions. On the road to Athlone an angry mob stoned the

preacher and his party, and knocked one of the group unconscious. Charles and his remaining companions rode back into
their midst just in time to prevent them completing their work
with a knife. A brave local woman who tried to intervene was
killed.

Many of the British soldiers stationed in Ireland responded
warmly to Charles's ministry, and forty dragoons were converted at St Philip's Town. In spite of the opposition his visit
was a great success and marked the continued growth of Irish
Methodism. Back in Dublin, Charles visited the prison, resulting in a condemned woman being reprieved as well as converted. With a touch of humour he reported that 'even the
Romish executioner was half converted'!

Charles and his companions pressed on, despite torn
clothes and bodies bruised by the mobs, poor lodgings, little
rest, and shortage of money. It was arranged for John to travel
across to Ireland and take over from Charles who, in the
spring of 1748, crossed the sea back to Holyhead.

Charles returned to Garth House, but only after a shocking
ride over the mountains through driving rain and in the face
of biting winds, as well as suffering a raging toothache. The
Gwynne family ran out to welcome him, but he was so physically shattered that they put him to bed and lovingly nursed
him for the best part of a week.

No sooner was he up than he was off again – this time to
Bristol, but during those few days the friendship between
Sarah and Charles quickly blossomed into true and lasting
love. Sarah and her father rode part of the way with Charles,
anxious to ensure that he was fit enough to ride to Bristol after
being so poorly. Sarah was doubly anxious to catch the last
possible glimpse of him, before he disappeared yet again. For
neither of them was it a case of 'out of sight out of mind';
Charles found himself constantly thinking about this charming, bright, sensible and spiritual young woman; while Sarah
was fully convinced that she would never meet another man

like Charles. He was different from other men she had met: conversation with him was relaxed and interesting. Their age difference did not seem to matter – she was twenty-one and he forty.

Sarah dreamed of their next meeting, as did Charles. Ten years had passed since General Oglethorpe in faraway Georgia had suggested to him that he ought to think about getting married. Occasionally he had gained the impression that one or two ladies rather fancied him, but the attraction was not mutual. With Sarah, however, it was different. Even when writing to her from Dublin in pastoral-style letters with details of his preaching activities, he could not help slipping in lines such as 'My heart is deeply engaged for you. . . .'

When back in England, in July 1748, Charles had the opportunity of entertaining Sarah and her father for six weeks. It was a time for all of them to get to know one another better. The first ten days were spent in Bristol, before Charles took them on to London for eighteen days, followed by three days in Oxford. They then returned to Bristol where Sarah got a sample of what lay ahead if she were to share her life with this man. She found herself awakened at 4 a.m. on the Sunday morning to be at Kingswood for the early Communion, followed by a round of four services in the fields, at which Charles preached. Then on to Bristol's famous Hotwells (where fashionable ladies listened from their carriages), before finishing up at the New Room in the Horse Fair, with singing and rejoicing until midnight. While all this activity was hectic and tiring, Sarah loved it. Most of all she knew that she really loved Charles, having had the opportunity to see him preaching.

It came to an end all too quickly for Sarah, but fortunately the parting was prolonged with Charles returning to Ireland via Garth House and a week of preaching in the area, before the painful farewell as she saw him ride off yet again to Holyhead for the Dublin ferry. Both of them now knew that they were in love and wanted to share the rest of their lives. She needed no persuading from Charles to write regularly, and he likewise. Their growing love was kept alive by the faithful keeping of their prayer trysts and their regular exchange of loving letters, with Charles now using 'Sally' as his special name for Sarah.

In Ireland Charles found himself increasingly popular, with thousands flocking to hear him, but he was more than ready when the time came for him to return to Wales. His father and mother were deceased, but he and John had a long-standing pact that neither would marry without consulting the other. So he arranged to discuss it with John. When they met it was no surprise for Charles to find that his brother – who could not resist organising everything, including his own life and Charles's – had already drawn up a shortlist of three 'eligible ladies'. Fortunately Sally's name was there and he expressed his immediate approval of Charles's choice. There was no problem with Sally's acceptance of Charles's proposal but he nervously anticipated difficulties with Mrs Gwynne, mainly over money, of which he had very little.

Sally and Charles discussed tactics when he arrived at Garth House and she wisely suggested that he put his proposal in a letter to her mother. This done, all he had to do was endure a weekend of waiting; but come Monday evening he knew he had to face the redoubtable Mrs Gwynne. To his delight and surprise she declared without hesitation that she would rather give her daughter to him than to any man in the country.

However, in the ensuing discussions, Mrs Gwynne raised several matters, two of which were money and Ireland. Charles reckoned he would be able to support Sally with £100 a year, which Mrs Gwynne felt was acceptable, though he had no firm idea as to how he was going to raise such a figure – small though it was to rich people like the Gwynnes. Charles and John had learned to live frugally and were givers not getters. It was John the organiser who came to the rescue with the suggestion that the money could be raised from the book-room sales of their writings, and especially Charles's hymns. They went into the matter with the printer who assured them that their writings were worth at least £2,500, which should be more than sufficient to raise £100 a year. Armed with this good news they returned in confident mood to face Mrs Gwynne, who proceeded to demolish their financial strategy with the uncompromising declaration that money dependent upon literature and hymns was unacceptable – only money backed by land would satisfy her. Marmaduke informed them that he was leaving the money matters in his wife's capable hands.

John and Charles with help from lawyer friends in London eventually managed to draw up a special bond, safeguarded by three trustees, which even Mrs Gwynne's keen financial brain could not fault. Indeed, when Sally's eldest brother, Howell (who was married to Lady Rudd), tried to raise objections to the match, his mother swiftly silenced him! Mrs Gwynne felt she had to ask Charles not to return to Ireland in view of the dangers he faced there; but she in turn was silenced when Sally bravely said that, if need be, she would accompany Charles to Ireland or anywhere else he felt he had to preach.

Charles confessed that he felt nearer to Sally than anyone he had ever met, but he feared he might disappoint her. After being a bachelor for so long how would he face up to mar-riage? This and other questions raced through his mind, but her letters calmed his fears and he eagerly anticipated the great day of their wedding, arranged for Saturday, 8th April 1749, at 8 p.m. in Llanlleonfel Church, with John officiating.

The spring day of the wedding was cloudless and Charles scribbled in his journal, 'Sweet day. . . .' Much of the day was spent in prayer and in the evening Charles led his beloved Sally into the church, where in a simple, solemn, yet deeply

happy service, John joined their hands together and pro-
nounced them man and wife. The register entry said, 'Charles
Wesley and Sarah Gwynne were lawfully married 8th April
1749.' The first lines of his hymn, written some two years
before, best describe their feelings:

> Love Divine, all loves excelling,
> Joy of Heaven to earth come down . . .

A few weeks after the wedding Sally had her first taste of
being married to a travelling preacher when Charles had to
leave her behind while he returned to Bristol, then went on to
London. It was two months before Sally was in his arms again.
Soon, however, they were house-hunting together in Bristol.
They selected 4 Charles Street, in the Stokes Croft area, to be
their home for the next twenty-two years. For a time Sally
accompanied Charles on every possible occasion and proved
a great travelling companion and a popular person with
Methodist societies everywhere. Sally's two spinster sisters,
Betsy and Peggy, also joined the household; and they were a
great help and comfort to Sally when Charles was away
preaching. Sally's skilled, loving care made Charles happy
and physically fitter than he had been for many years. They
were overjoyed when Sally experienced her first pregnancy;
but this turned to sadness when she suffered a miscarriage.

Meanwhile Methodism continued to thrive, but growth
meant more problems, burdens and travelling. However, in
spite of all the pressures Charles and Sally's love prospered
and soon they were rejoicing in the birth of a son, Jackie.

Charles was called urgently to London where John was ill
with galloping consumption and not expected to live; he got
so low that he wrote his own epitaph, but the anticipated
funeral was postponed for some forty years when God most
wonderfully raised him up and restored his health. Charles's
joy over John's amazing recovery was cut short by news that

at home in Bristol Sally was laid low with the dreaded small-pox and her life was in danger.

Charles hurried home, dreading that he might lose her and reproaching himself for being absent when she needed him badly. For three agonising weeks the illness raged, but many prayed for her and she recovered. However, she knew only too well the after-effects of smallpox and plucking up her courage she looked into her hand mirror and gasped in horror at the pock-marked face that confronted her. No one would ever again suggest that she was beautiful. Even more important – would Charles still love her? She was only too aware of other young wives who had been robbed not only of their good looks by the curse of smallpox, but, in effect, of their marriages too. These fears left her as soon as Charles took her in his arms, hugging her closely to him and looking into her tear-filled eyes, not only assuring her of his undying love, but also declaring that this made him love her more than ever.

Duty called Charles back to London where urgent prob-lems in the societies demanded his presence. Sally's health and strength had recovered sufficiently for her to be up from her sickbed, only for tragedy to strike again: baby Jackie, just sixteen months old, developed smallpox. A letter was sent to Charles but Jackie died and was buried before Charles reached Bristol. Again their love was tested to the limits, only to emerge deepened and widened by yet another trial. In all they had eight children but only three survived. The three sur-vivors – Charles, Sally and Samuel – were a great comfort and joy to Sally and helped to fill the many lonely hours she faced with Charles busier and his ministry more blessed than ever.

Charles was never too busy to write, however. In his letters he repeatedly expressed his love for Sally with such phrases as 'My heart is with you. . . . No one can supply your place.' He usually opened with 'My Dearest of Creatures' and wisely urged her with such things as 'do not neglect your music . . . or your shorthand . . . or your prayers'. Sally was equally faithful with her letters, and if one was late or missed, Charles felt cast down. Thanks largely to Sally, her two sons and daughter were musically gifted and, in spite of always being short of funds, Charles somehow found money to purchase a harpsichord for them and to pay for music lessons.

Charles was increasingly concerned about the amount of time he was compelled to spend away from home. The problem was solved in 1771 with a move to London, where the society at the 'Foundery' (refurbished as a preaching place) was demanding more and more of his time. John agreed and, although Charles was also committed to visiting Bristol regularly, it meant that at last he would be able to spend more time with his family. Thanks to the help of a kind friend they were able to move into a suitable house, fully furnished, in Great Chesterfield Street.

The next seventeen years were the most settled, happiest years of Charles and Sally's lives, and young Charles and Samuel were now displaying outstanding talent with their music. Sally enjoyed having Charles at home so much of the time, with the long journeys virtually over. Charles's health benefited and he became a familiar sight in the area as he rode the three miles to the new City Road Chapel, opened in 1778. The area around their home was still quite rural and while out riding on his mare he frequently composed hymns, as well as suddenly bursting into joyous singing.

Charles was now feeling his age, but he was growing old gracefully and enjoying these more tranquil years with his beloved Sally and their musically gifted sons and daughter Sarah. Young Charles's and Samuel's prodigious musical talent attracted both royal and London society's attention. It was obvious to the family in the early days of spring 1788 that Charles had not long to live, but death (which had once succeeded in frightening him and John on the storm-tossed ship bound for Georgia) had long since lost all its terrors. When a visitor suggested that death's valley was hard to pass through, he replied very smartly, 'Not with Christ.' Two days before the end he dictated to his dear Sally another hymn, the third and fourth lines of which were as follows:

> Jesus my only Hope Thou art,
> Strength of my failing flesh and heart.

On 29th March, his last morning on earth, Sally tenderly took hold of his hand and bending over him asked him to press if he could hear her. (Earlier when she asked if he had anything to say, he managed to open his eyes and respond, 'Only thanks, love . . . Blessing.') He now mustered just enough strength for a very feeble little squeeze, accompanied by a whispered, 'Lord – my heart – my God.' Shortly afterwards he breathed his last peaceful breath. He was buried in the church graveyard of Old Marylebone.

It was another thirty-five years before she joined him in that quiet graveyard. As the last three lines of his immortal hymn 'Love Divine' say:

> . . . Till in heaven we take our place,
> Till we cast our crowns before Thee,
> Lost in wonder, love, and praise.

# 3
# William and Catherine Booth

Their unlikely romance budded and bloomed during a short journey in a Victorian horse-drawn cab. What happened in that old cab was so remarkable that they remembered every moment of it for the rest of their eventful lives.

The cabby had been called by boot manufacturer Edward Harris Rabbits, a prosperous businessman. All hope of a generous tip vanished when the cabby was instructed, 'Now my good man, I want you to take two friends of mine to Brixton. And mind you drive steadily: the young lady started to feel unwell this afternoon during our special Good Friday services. But don't look so worried; the young man escorting her home is one of our best preachers, and I have instructed him to take good care of her.'

High up on his perch the cabby watched his prospective fares emerge from the Cowper Street schoolroom where the Methodist Reformers were holding their Easter services. Diminutive and delicate, she appeared fragile, and was leaning for obviously needed support on the arm of a tall but painfully thin young man. She struggled bravely to the cab, but still managed a wan smile for the cabby and a caring look at his tired old horse. Her pale face spoke of suffering but her warm dark eyes somehow enhanced her features.

As for the young man, he was so tall – over six feet – that his head was level with the top of the cab, revealing to the cabby a thin, impressive face, topped with a mop of black hair. His neatly trimmed beard stretched from ear to ear round a firm chin, but his upper lip was clean shaven. His dramatic appearance was enhanced by a large hooked nose, but his striking grey eyes redeemed the gaunt face from being forbidding. As he looked up at the cabby, having gently helped the unwell young lady into her seat, his kind eyes made the cabby feel that he was regarded as an equal and appreciated as a fellow human being.

Mr Rabbits saw the cab safely on its way before turning back into the Cowper Street schoolroom for the evening service. He reflected about the well-being of his two young friends. He was very concerned about Miss Catherine Mumford, for whom he had the highest regard. His acquaintance with the family stretched back over several years, starting soon after the Mumfords had moved to London from Boston, Lincolnshire. Her father, John, was a fairly successful carriage-builder. Sarah, her mother, was a fine, capable woman, a devout Methodist, and a devoted, caring and loving mother to her gifted but constantly ailing daughter. Sarah, sadly, had lost three tiny baby sons in succession, before giving birth to Catherine twenty-three years before. Mentally her daughter was bright. Unaided, she had learned the alphabet and was reading by the age of three. Spiritually, she was outstanding and mature beyond her years. So much so that Mr Rabbits put great store upon Catherine's opinion on religious matters, especially about preachers.

It was Catherine's opinion about the preaching ability of the young William Booth that had confirmed his own estimate and convinced him that he should support him financially for a probationary period of three months. William had moved down to London from Nottingham over a year before, seeking work. As a Methodist lay preacher he was given opportunities to preach. And that was how Mr Rabbits first heard him, immediately realising that here was a special talent worth encouraging. Catherine Mumford had also been in that service. Afterwards Mr Rabbits asked her opinion of Mr Booth's preaching, and she replied without hesitation that she thought it was the best preaching she had heard in the church for some time, and that more preaching like that would soon bring revival. Mr Rabbits couldn't have agreed more; his desire to see Methodism revived was why he had joined the Reformed Methodists. This was the kind of preaching his church needed. He had arranged a meeting with William and the interview served to increase his confidence in the character and commitment of the young preacher.

Now almost twenty-three years of age, William had been born in Nottingham. After some prosperous years, his father's modest building business was in difficulties; the calling in of a mortgage meant that they had to move to a smaller house, and plans for William's education at the widely acclaimed Mr Biddulph's School had to be abandoned. When William was thirteen years old his father died 'of shock', but not before he had apprenticed his son to Frances Eames, pawnbroker.

The Battle of Waterloo in 1815 was a great victory for the nation. However, the years that followed were increasingly difficult for multitudes of the poorer people, who were not helped by the imposition of bad taxes, and the Corn Laws, which kept bread prices high. The accession of the young Queen Victoria at the age of eighteen on 20th June 1837 brought no immediate relief. She married Albert in 1840, but the monarchy was unpopular due to the excesses of George IV and his brothers.

During the 'hungry-1840s' William, in the pawnbroker's shop, came face to face with poverty, and it deeply moved and challenged his young heart. Briefly he flirted with the Chartists, who were seeking to help the poor by political change. He and his three sisters had been brought up to attend church, and he was attracted to the warm atmosphere of the services at the Wesleyan chapel on Broad Street. While he was walking home from a meeting late one evening in 1844 he became converted. He had been under conviction for some time, mainly because of the way he had deceived a few friends by some clever transactions, for the 'benefits' of which they presented him with a silver pencil case as a token of appreciation. He knew he had to confess his deception to them and return the gift, no matter what the cost. His repentance was from the heart and there, alone on the street, he knew that Christ had met with him, just as the Saviour had met with his hero John Wesley. William's heart too 'was strangely warmed', and a profound change came over him. At the first opportunity he confessed to his friends and returned the silver pencil case. Within days he was preaching Christ on the streets. The stirring ministry of visiting revivalists to Broad Street Chapel helped him and he was a quick and eager learner, but none inspired him more than the highly successful Irish-American Methodist evangelist, the Revd James Caughey. Soon William's one ambition in life was to win the lost for Christ – he saw this as the only real solution for the poor, and the only thing that truly mattered.

Edward Rabbits was convinced that he had made the right decision to support William for three months. And what of Catherine Mumford? Such a gifted young lady; it was a great shame about her chronic ill health – if only she were stronger. As Rabbits settled into his seat for the evening Good Friday service, he could not help but wonder how the two of them were faring on the cab drive home.

In fact, they were faring very well. Within minutes they were engaged in the warmest conversation as though they had known each other for years, whereas this was only their third meeting and the first time they had been alone together. There was an immediate rapport between them; they felt at ease with each other and the more they exchanged their views and experiences, the closer their souls seemed knit together. There was no physical contact between them, however, not even holding of hands, as this was Victorian England. But a unity that was destined to last was established between them in the few miles of the ride to Brixton.

Years later, Catherine described that ride:

> That little journey will never be forgotten by either of us. It is true that nothing particular occurred, except that as William after-wards expressed it, it seemed as if God flashed simultaneously into our hearts that affection which afterwards ripened into what has proved at least to be an exceptional union of heart and purpose and life, and which none of the changing vicissitudes with which our lives have been so crowded has been able to efface.
>
> I had been introduced to him as being in delicate health, and he took the situation in at a glance. His thought for me, although such a stranger, appeared most remarkable. The conveyance shook me; he regretted it. The talking exhausted me; he saw and forbade it. And then we struck in at once in such wonderful harmony of view and aim and feeling on varied matters that passed rapidly before us. It seemed as though we had intimately known and loved each other for years, and suddenly, after some temporary absence, had been brought together again, and before we reached my home we both suspected, nay, we felt as though we had been made for each other, and that henceforth the current of our lives must flow together.[1]

At the end of that short but memorable journey, William gently helped Catherine out of the carriage. The cabby watched them as they walked to the front door of Catherine's home and sensed something was different about them, but didn't know what exactly. The young lady certainly seemed a lot more sprightly than when she had begun the journey. Now, she was not so much leaning on the young man's arm as holding it, and there was almost a spring in her step. What had happened in his cab, he could not be sure – all that had passed between them was words. He touched his cap as they

---

[1] Roger J. Green, *Catherine Booth* (Monarch 1997), p. 44.

turned and said, 'Goodnight and thank you. God bless you.'
As he took up the reins and moved off, he could not help but
wonder whether they were falling in love. However, neither
looked robust, and if they were in love, he couldn't see much
of a future for them: the young lady was obviously in poor
health and as for the young man, he was so thin that it looked
as though a puff of wind could blow him over. Little did he
realise that he had witnessed the beginning of what one
highly respected writer described as 'one of the most remarkable and charming love stories in the world'.[2]

Having arrived home earlier than expected, Catherine
assured her fussing, anxious mother that she had not stayed
until the evening service because of feeling unwell, but was
now quite recovered – thanks, in part, to Mr Booth who, at Mr
Rabbits's request, had kindly escorted her home. Mrs
Mumford had heard and liked Mr Booth's preaching and she
welcomed him into her gracious home. That over with,
Catherine and William seated themselves on the sofa and took
up their talking where it had had to break off in the cab. In
Catherine's own words, 'The conversation was lively and
interesting, and my mother listened and had her say.'

They both wanted to know everything about each other,
and in response to an endless succession of questions the
stories of their lives came pouring out in an excited torrent.
Every precious detail seemed to dovetail together perfectly.
Surely this fashioning of their two lives had to be the work of
the Lord Jesus, 'the Master Carpenter'?

What excitement when William discovered that Catherine
was born in Ashbourne, Derbyshire, slightly over twenty
miles from his Nottingham. (The Mumfords had moved to
Boston, Lincolnshire, in 1834, hoping it would benefit
Catherine's health.) Her mother told a story of when

---

[2] Harold Begbie, *The Life of General William Booth* (Macmillan 1920).

Catherine was twelve years old. She was playing on the street with her hoop and stick – bowling it along – when close by, a policeman suddenly darted out of an alley and arrested a barefooted tramp right in front of her. A merry crowd, pouring out of a pub to enjoy the fun, taunted and jeered the down-and-out prisoner. Their cruel taunts so got to young Catherine that without more ado she marched alongside the wretch all the way to the police station. Her kind action silenced the drunken jeers. As he was shoved roughly inside to the cells, the ragged man turned and gave young Catherine a sad smile of thanks she was never able to forget.

Many such stories continued from Mrs Mumford. Her Catherine not only cared about people in need, but also had a caring heart for animals – and woe betide anyone she came across ill-treating an animal. Even as a little girl she was not afraid to confront and rebuke a person she found being cruel to any animal – be it a horse, a donkey, a dog or a cat.

The conversation never flagged – William and Catherine wanted to find out everything they could about each other; and Mother was also keen to know more about this young man, to whom her daughter was clearly attracted. Her motherly concern made sure that William was well acquainted with her battles with Catherine's many illnesses, which included such formidable foes as tuberculosis and curvature of the spine. These had limited her formal schooling to a brief two-year spell; Catherine's wide knowledge was due to her love of reading: she had read the Bible through eight times before she was a teenager; she revelled in theology, appreciated the classics, and was an avid letter writer. Her mother ensured she had a constant supply of good books (no novels allowed), and did her utmost to further Catherine's education at home.

William found himself having to unfold more of his own life-story. He mentioned that the Methodists had not renewed his 'class-ticket' (a term from John Wesley's days), without which he was no longer a member. On moving to London

William joined Walworth Chapel, to which he was also attached as a lay preacher. The respectable, well-to-do Methodists who constituted most of the congregation did not find his fire and brimstone preaching to their liking. Seeing the crowds of people who frequented the nearby Kennington Common, William started preaching there (after the style of John Wesley and George Whitefield). He was in his element as he was a born evangelist. But it embarrassed the church leaders and they requested him to stop his open-air preaching on the Common. He refused. They needed no more to convince them that he must be one of those troublesome 'Methodist Reformers' and at the end of the quarter, the chapel stewards would not renew his membership.

Catherine, too, had suffered the indignity of not having her class-ticket renewed. This was because of her sympathy and open support for the Reformers with their emphasis on soul-winning, holiness, and the Holy Spirit's empowerment for ministry. She and William were fellow sufferers and kindred spirits.

One Sunday evening in 1846, when William was still in Nottingham, he had gathered together a crowd from Nottingham's worst slums, and brought them triumphantly into Broad Street Chapel, through the main door. He ushered them into the best seats, facing the pulpit, normally occupied only by 'pewholders'. The businessmen, managers, shop owners and their well-attired wives were affronted at this latest exploit of Wilful Will, as many had nicknamed him. It was established custom that the poor – if ever they came to chapel – used another door and were 'kept apart' on backless and cushionless benches behind a partition that screened off the pulpit. Children, it was said, should be seen and not heard. But the poor, it seems, should be neither seen nor heard. William was oblivious to all this; he was thrilled at having succeeded in bringing this crowd of poor sinners into the house of God. He had a gift for music and loved to sing the great hymns; that night he sang with greater gusto than usual. Ignorance is bliss, but his blissful ignorance of the attitude that had taken over respectable Methodism was soon shattered. After the service he was summoned before the deacons and the minister and told that in future such people must enter by the side door and sit in their appointed seats. William could not understand their attitude. He had had the joy of seeing some of the worst characters in Nottingham's slums gloriously converted and wonderfully changed: people like Besom Jack, a drunken broom-seller, who found Christ as his Saviour right there on the street through William's preaching and became one of his most faithful followers. He was only one of many such 'changed rogues', real conversions, the living proofs of William's calling as an evangelist.

On and on Catherine and William talked, story following story until William glanced up at the clock and was startled to realise how late it was – the time had flown by with the precious sharing of their backgrounds. He got up to go and asked if his hosts would kindly excuse him; it had been a wonderful evening and it had made it a wonderful birthday for him, but he really had to go. When Catherine discovered that they were both born in 1829, she in January, he in April, she felt a further bond between them.

When she found out that William faced a long walk to his destination, Mrs Mumford insisted he stay the night with them; after all, he had been kind enough to see her daughter safely home.

William explained that he was used to walking long distances. Since coming to London, he found to his bitter disappointment that the only job he could get was with another pawnbroker. He had not believed it possible, but this one turned out to be even meaner than his Nottingham counterpart. William often had to run home to avoid being locked out. He explained that his quarters were above the pawnbroker's shop and his employer always shut the doors promptly at 10 p.m. on Sunday nights. William frequently found himself preaching up to eight miles away, which often meant that he had to run much of the way back to get in before lock-up time. Catherine pictured him pounding across that part of London in the dark night, his long legs covering the ground in great strides, breathing hard (obviously no athlete) – exhausted and weary after preaching with the energy she had seen him employ when in the pulpit. She was relieved and delighted when William told her he had been able to give his notice to leave the pawnbroker thanks to Mr Rabbits, and would soon be free to concentrate on preaching.

Mrs Mumford insisted that he stay the night in the spare room. William accepted and Catherine breathed a contented sigh – what a wonderful day it had been. Surely God had brought them together. She felt more and more sure of that, although there were still some important things she knew she must discuss with him. However, no sooner had William closed the bedroom door of the pleasant guest room, than the euphoria of meeting this wonderful and amazingly like-minded young lady suddenly deserted him as a whole battalion of bewildering doubts clamoured to be heard. He knew that he was falling head over heels in love with Catherine; but how could he contemplate any thoughts of their future together? He had only just got the release he yearned for from the grinding tyranny of the pawnbroker's, through the generosity of his new-found friend and sponsor, Mr Rabbits. The prospect of being totally free to concentrate on preaching and seeking to bring the lost to Christ every day of the week was a dream come true. His supreme desire was the will of God for his life. How could he even think of marriage? Mr Rabbits had been generous. When he had asked William how much he needed to live on, William had said he was sure he could manage on 12s 6d per week. Mr Rabbits dismissed that as insufficient and insisted on supporting his new protégé with one pound a week. William was delighted as he had scraped a living for most of his teenage years, trying to support his widowed mother and his three sisters. To do so he had eaten frugally, the food often poor, which on top of his being over-worked had been a factor in his chronic dyspepsia. Though he hated pawn-broking he knew he had been a good employee. In Nottingham soon after his conversion he had told his employer, Mr Eames, that he was no longer willing to work after midnight on Saturday evening: Sunday was the Lord's Day. Mr Eames had sacked him, but soon found he could not do without him and had to face the humiliation of asking William to return. However, when the young man's five-year apprenticeship was completed he lost his job because Mr Eames claimed he could not afford to pay a higher wage. William knew that he had been a good worker, but money had no attraction as such – his one burning desire was to win souls. When he was only sixteen he wrote, 'What is the hope of money-earning in comparison with the imperishable wealth of ingathered souls?'

By the time morning came doubts and fears had taken over. In his heart he knew he loved Catherine, and was equally certain that she loved him, but love and the future had not been men-tioned. The more he thought about it, the more despondent he became. How could he, in his threadbare financial circumstances, care adequately for Catherine with her precarious health?

So it was that he left the Mumfords' comfortable home feeling troubled in spirit. The perfect woman had been pre-sented to him, only for him to have to surrender her to the gloomy prospects of never being able – in the foreseeable future – to provide her with the care she needed and deserved. He also knew that no matter what the cost he dare not, would not, could not, turn from the path of God's will for his life as he saw it. Already the future seemed so much darker after his having experienced those few precious hours full of light and hope, which her presence had radiated into his life.

It was an equally testing time for Catherine although, because of her temperament, she dealt with it rather differently. When she was not quite sixteen years of age she had experienced a friendship with an intelligent, attractive young man, a lifelong acquaintance of the family. But as the weeks passed she discovered that he was not a committed Christian and, although he was fond of her as she was of him, she could not get away from the voice of her conscience which kept reminding her of God's word on such matters, 'Do not be yoked together with unbelievers' (2 Corinthians 6:14). It was a searching time, but eventually she knew that she had to end this relationship.

While still a teenager she had set out her requirements for a husband, if ever the case should arise:

> He must be a sincere Christian, not a nominal one, or a mere church member, but truly converted to God. He must be a man of sense – I know that I could never respect a fool, or one much weaker mentally than myself. He must be a total abstainer – and this from conviction and not merely to gratify me.[3]

She also decided that 'he should be a minister – I could be most useful to God as a minister's wife'. As an interesting extra she added, 'He should be dark, tall and for preference called William.' After William's mournful departure that morning, she was left wondering and waiting. Surely she was not mistaken – she had felt such an assurance that he was the one with whom she was to share her life.

Within a matter of hours William returned to the Mumfords' home. He could not keep away; he had to see her and open his heart to her and explain his financial situation. Over the next few weeks they met almost daily and talked and prayed through all the obstacles that seemed to block their future. They agreed that nothing must be done in haste. It was then that William discovered the depths of Catherine's commitment to Christ. Before she would accept any pledge of his love he must first be convinced in his own mind that it was God's will.

---

[3] Roger J. Green, *Catherine Booth*, p. 57.

It was an extremely difficult month for both of them, with a great deal of heart searching, lots of praying, and frank exchanges. Their situation was not eased either when Mrs Mumford made it clear by her attitude that she was far from persuaded about William's suitability in view of his poor financial circumstances and his uncertain future. But though Catherine listened to her mother, she knew that this was something that had to be settled between William and herself. They were both adults and established Christians. As well as talking they exchanged letters – Catherine especially found it helpful to express her faith and feelings in writing. William declared his love for her, but both were prepared to surrender their friendship if this was discovered as being God's will.

After a month of agonising they were finally persuaded that their future was to be together and on 13th May 1852 they knelt side by side before the sofa in Catherine's home. Hand joined to loving hand they prayed and solemnly gave themselves to each other and to God. It was so special that almost a year later Catherine wrote about it to her beloved William, who was a hundred miles away in Spalding, Lincolnshire:

> We are one in all things; it will be twelve months on the 13th May since, bowed together at this sofa, we solemnly gave ourselves to each other and to God. If you will, we will always keep this as our real wedding day. It was so in the sight of God and in all the highest and holiest senses, the next is a mere legal knot, that was a moral and spiritual union of souls.[4]

At the end of his three months of support by Mr Rabbits, after a cruel spell of waiting and seeking for the right opening, William was given charge of the Reformers' Spalding circuit. The next eighteen months he spent all his energies on building up his twenty-seven mile wide parish, criss-crossing

---

[4] *Ibid.*, p. 302.

much of it on foot, or rattling over the flat fenlands in a horse-drawn gig. His preaching was well received and he had the joy of seeing many respond to his appeals to 'receive Christ as Saviour and Lord'. Never one to spare himself, he drove himself unmercifully, preaching many times every week, over-working, and over-eating as the farming community plied him with more food than he had ever been used to, and more than was good for him late at night after preaching, followed frequently by a long walk or drive back to his lodgings.

Trains were still in their infancy and Spalding was not only another county; it was almost as though William was in another country – timewise it was two days' journey away. Catherine wrote almost every day, but William was too busy to reciprocate with the same regularity and by no means could he manage the same length of letter. Catherine's loving, caring letters bridged the many miles that kept them apart. In her letters she urged him to conserve his energies, pressing him not to allow the chapel leaders to take advantage of his willingness and eagerness to preach whenever asked, and cajoling him to plan his schedule to include time for much-needed study and reading. They were true love-letters of the highest quality and William, though hard-pressed to respond as frequently and as fully as his beloved asked him to, valued and appreciated her letters more than he could ever fully express.

The nearest they ever got to a lovers' tiff was over one of Catherine's strongest causes: the equality of the sexes. Women's rights were something she had researched and supported for years. When a fairly prominent minister was publicly dismissive of 'the weaker sex' and disparaging about their lesser abilities and inferior roles, Catherine wrote a blistering reply and sent a copy to William in Spalding, trusting to receive his whole-hearted support. She was mortified and enraged when William sided with the minister. Her next letter told William exactly how she felt, and challenged, 'I am sure no one can prove it [woman's inferiority to man] from the word of God.' Shaken and duly chastened William replied with a conciliatory gesture, which still came across as patronising (he had much to learn about the latent abilities of his beloved Catherine), 'I would not encourage a woman to begin preaching . . . although I would not stop her on any account. . . . I would not stop you if I had power to do so, although I should not like it.' A few years into the future he would be tested on that statement.

William missed Catherine terribly, but was content with his lot in Spalding; his success was appreciated by the good folk there, but on one of his all-too-rare visits to Catherine in London they faced up to reality. After more talks and more letters, Catherine's clear-headedness focused on the core issue. If William were ever to become a fully ordained minister of the Free Churches he would have to complete a course in a training college. Catherine had been doing her homework and discovered that there was a special course run by another breakaway group, the Methodist New Connexion, in Camberwell, under Revd Dr William Cooke. William applied for the course and was accepted.

It was hard going. William was intelligent and had many talents, but he was never cut out to be an academic. Learning Greek and Latin he found to be a real chore, and Dr Cooke kept his students so busy that he actually saw even less of Catherine. Fortunately, Dr Cooke was a wise and discerning person. When William preached in Brunswick Chapel on the day of his enrolment, there were fifteen converts.

Dr Cooke observed him carefully and when his own daughter was brought to the Saviour through William's preaching, he knew that William's destiny did not depend on scholasticism.

William and Catherine were married at Stockwell New Chapel on 16th June 1855. It was a small but special wedding. Beforehand Catherine wrote to William:

I read the Marriage Service and wept over it. Because others go and swear in the presence of God to . . . fulfil certain conditions, without even reflecting on their nature and extent, that is no reason why I should do so. No, I should go to the altar with a full sense of what I am doing and an awful view of its consequences through all time, nay, far beyond![5]

The only family members present were William's sister, Emma, and Catherine's father, John. Their honeymoon of one week was spent at Ryde on the Isle of Wight; but the second week of their married life was spent in Guernsey where an evangelistic campaign had been arranged. On the short sea journey Catherine was seasick and was unable to attend William's crowded and successful campaign.

William was becoming known as a highly successful evangelist and his next campaign was in York; unfortunately Catherine was still too ill to travel with him and spent the time with her parents in their home. She managed to travel to Hull to be there with William for his next campaign; the meetings were crowded and there were some three hundred conversions. But her poor health made her feel very dispirited; she wanted to be with William and support him as much as possible, but clearly she was going to find the constant travelling extremely difficult – in fact, almost impossible. Hull was the home town of the famous reformer William Wilberforce, and a woman choir member who had known him personally told Catherine, 'That little shrimp was God's man. Here is a copy of his biography. Read it.' She did and was amazed and encouraged to discover that Wilberforce had been described as a 'living corpse', suffering with a crooked back and bad health; but he overcame these handicaps and the bitter opposition his anti-slavery bill provoked. The book was the inspiration she needed at that critical time and as she sought God in prayer she gained a new confidence. She determined to be in William's next service and

---

[5] Catherine Bramwell Booth, *Catherine Booth: The Story of Her Loves* (Hodder 1970).

quoted the text God had quickened to her from Psalm 27:1, 'The Lord is the strength of my life.' William hugged her to him and whispered in her ear, 'Kate [his favourite pet name for Catherine], my dear, I love you more every day.'

Catherine's health improved but she was destined to battle with her physical weaknesses all her life. However, she never allowed them to stop her, and with William, in the course of time, succeeded in founding The Salvation Army. She became the mother of eight wonderful children, many of them destined to leave their lasting mark on the world in their sacrificial service for Christ. For her, with her poor health, to produce such a large, happy, dedicated and talented family seemed an impossible dream. But then to become a great speaker and evangelist herself, as well as a gifted writer and pioneer of women's rights!

However, in 1855 all that was still in the distant future. In 1856 when they were based in Halifax with the Methodist New Connexion, they welcomed the birth of their first child, a beautiful baby boy – William Bramwell Booth – destined in the next century to succeed his father as General of The Salvation Army. In 1857 they were in the Brighouse circuit, where their second son, Ballington, was born on 28th July. The next year, 1858, saw them in charge of the Gateshead circuit, where their first daughter, Catherine, was born on 18th September. That these children were born in such rapid succession, and not only survived but thrived, is amazing in itself, considering the number of children in those days who died in infancy. Catherine, when the mother of two children, said, 'It seems too much to be true, that they are so healthy when I am such a poor thing.' In Gateshead, after the birth of their first daughter, Catherine remarked to William that she had been working out how long it had taken them to produce their first three children: just 31 months and 10 days. Even more remarkable is the fact that all but one of their eight children lived to be old (Emma, the exception, was killed in a train crash in 1903).

It was also in Gateshead that Catherine – just one year after the birth of baby Catherine – made history. The year 1859 was a period of revival. Igniting in America in 1857, the fire spread to the UK via Ireland, and thence to Scotland and England. An American couple, Dr and Mrs Palmer, were ministering with outstanding results in Newcastle and Mrs Palmer was a far more effective preacher than her husband. This roused the indignation of a minister in nearby Sunderland who published a pamphlet denouncing women preachers. Catherine knew she had to set about writing a comprehensive rebuttal. All her personal convictions, fortified by many years of researching this controversial subject, were poured eloquently and logically into a thirty-two page pamphlet, *Female Ministry*. William backed her with this project and it provoked furious debate. Male chauvinism ruled in Victorian England; women did not have a vote; educationally they were treated as inferior and barred from the higher learning establishments, as well as from many of the professions; but, in Catherine's eyes, worse still was the unequal treatment of women preachers by the churches. Her reply was solely on the grounds of principle and the Scriptures. She had no thought of becoming a preacher herself.

The eventful year of 1860 began with the birth of their second daughter, Emma, on 8th January. Catherine was never happier. Writing home she said, 'William was never more tender or more loving or more attentive than now. He often tells me I grow more beautiful in his sight and more precious to his heart day by day.'

With her new baby daughter in her arms she found herself thinking back to her conversion at seventeen years of age, when after several years of uncertainty she finally found the assurance of salvation she yearned for. The reading of Charles Wesley's account in his journal of his own conversion greatly helped her. She realised that all God asked of her was to believe and rest on his word. There and then she made a fresh resolve that she would be obedient to any further promptings of the Holy Spirit. On Whit Sunday William was on the point of closing the service in the packed church (capable of seating 1,250 people). Catherine was sitting in the minister's pew with four-year-old Bramwell when she 'felt the Holy Spirit come upon her'. She had forgotten her vow, but was soon reminded of it by the Spirit of God. She made the momentous decision to obey despite the outcome and, rising from her seat, walked down the aisle towards the pulpit. Every eye watched and wondered. They all loved her, but knew her only as being a very timid person. William saw her coming towards him and went to meet her, anxious lest she had been taken ill. 'What is the matter, my dear?' 'I want to say a word.' William was taken aback but recovered quickly to announce, 'My dear wife wants to say a word.'

Catherine had everyone's attention with her first sentence: 'I want to confess that I have been disobedient to the Holy Spirit about speaking.' After a few moving sentences many were in tears: she was touching their hearts. As soon as she had finished William told them, 'Mrs Booth will be preaching here this evening.' The news quickly spread and it was to an even greater congregation – with young people perched on window ledges around the large church – that Catherine stood and announced her text, 'Be filled with the Spirit.' Her ministry was very warmly received. It was the beginning of her role as one of the most outstanding speakers – male or female – of her day. Soon invitations were flooding in for her to preach in chapels around the area. The first Sunday in June she preached with great acceptance in Newcastle. But then William fell ill with a severe throat infection and was forced to rest at home. There was only one thing for it – Catherine would have to take his place in the church, which she did with great success. William was thrilled; all his reservations about women's ministry had been banished. He was more than happy with their reversed roles – he at home looking after the children, and

Catherine occupying the pulpit. William's illness dragged on and he had to go away for complete rest, during which Catherine's preaching was taking Gateshead by storm.

Although William was successful as a circuit minister he longed to be freed to fulfil his real ministry as an evangelist. Catherine backed him to the hilt, even though she trembled at the prospect of returning to the constant travelling and the unsettled life of an evangelist's wife, as well as the periods when they would of necessity be separated for days and weeks at a time. The 1861 Conference at Liverpool turned down William's request to be released to be a full-time evangelist. Within a month William resigned from the Methodist New Connexion to become a freelance evangelist. It was a daring step of faith, but one that Catherine fully endorsed – even though she knew it would impose great financial pressures upon them with their rapidly growing family. Their task was not made any easier when the Connexion leaders forbade any of their churches to engage him for campaigns. The strain was tremendous but their love for each other and their mutual support never wavered.

Then, risking the wrath of the church authorities, a young minister (a convert of William's) invited William to his church in Cornwall for a campaign. He told them frankly that he could not promise much – his congregation was small – but if William was willing he could come for a two-week campaign. God so owned the ministry of William and Catherine that the whole county was stirred; it was a period of revival with thousands attending and some seven thousand brought to Christ. The two weeks became eighteen wonderful and never-to-be-forgotten months. Also memorable was the birth of another son, Herbert Howard, on 26th August 1862 in Penzance.

More successful campaigns followed and in spite of the hectic life, William and Catherine continued to stimulate and challenge each other to ever greater heights in God and ever increasing love and respect for each other. Another daughter, Marian Billups, was born on 4th May 1864 in Leeds.

Catherine had a strong desire to return to London. In July 1865 William was asked to conduct a tent campaign in the East End of London. It was a great success in spite of the tent leaking badly in the wet weather before collapsing: opponents of the campaign quite possibly cut the ropes!

After the campaign moved to New Road, Whitechapel, William burst in on Catherine one evening with the staggering declaration, 'Darling, I have found my destiny. Where can I find such heathen as these?' Catherine had her doubts: they were in debt, and with six children the prospects of labouring in such a rough and poverty-stricken area of London with its cockfighting, opium dens, prostitution and gin palaces by the score were daunting indeed.

It was a challenge that few could have faced. It took all their courage, faith and love for Christ, for each other, and for the needy 'heathen' of London's East End, but history has confirmed the correctness of their decision. In 1865 they formed the Christian Revival Association (later the Christian Mission). Then, in 1878, this became The Salvation Army, the amazing growth of which is well documented and accepted as unique in the history of the Christian church.

The terrible battles they faced are daunting even to read about. Brewers organised violent mobs to intimidate them, the worst being in Sheffield when many Salvationists – women as well as men – were attacked with clubs and stones and foully abused. Their social work coupled with their soul-saving evangelism and rescue work has circled the globe and now has the respect of the world.

Catherine's preaching ministry went from strength to strength. She filled the most famous halls around the nation, and won not only many converts to Christ, but many supporters for The Salvation Army. William mercilessly drove himself on and on, never sparing himself. He caught typhoid but recovered to continue fighting the good fight. However, the greatest blow of his life struck in 1888 when it was diagnosed that his beloved Catherine's swelling on her breast was malignant and needed immediate surgery. Success could not be guaranteed and he was told that without the operation her life expectancy was two years at the most. (Catherine's mother had died with the same malignancy in 1869.) Every possible avenue of help was explored, but in vain. Much prayer was made for her and people needed no urging to intercede because she held a unique place in so many of their hearts. William cried out in agony, 'Oh God, help just now; help my darling!' With the kind and generous help of rich benefactors it was made possible for Catherine to spend her last days near the sea at Clacton. Though in almost constant pain she received her family and countless friends over the months. Several times the doctors thought she was going to die, but she revived again.

Meanwhile, the growing work of The Salvation Army had to go on. William was busy writing what was the expression of his heart's concern for the poor. In spite of her pain Catherine read it and suggested improvements, and encouraged William in his writing of what was destined to become a best-seller (all the profits going back into Salvation Army funds). It was entitled *Darkest England and the Way Out*. It was a far-seeing programme of social reform that was decades ahead of the thinking of any political group. To the end William and Catherine's love for each other continued to grow deeper and more wonderful.

Catherine's 'promotion to glory' came on 4th October 1890. William missed her terribly but laboured on until his own death on 20th August 1912. William and Catherine Booth reached greater heights in their lives together than they ever could have as individuals. They proved to each other and to a doubting world that Christian marriage is a divine institution that will never be bettered in this life.

# 4
# *Smith and Polly Wigglesworth*

It was love at first shout, rather than love at first sight, although the young lady had already caught the shy young plumber's attention – she was pleasing to the eyes as well as the ears.

The scene took place in a rundown old theatre in booming Bradford in 1877. However, Act One of this real-life romance occurred not on the stage but in the stalls. It was the first time pretty young Polly, aged only seventeen years, had ever dared to venture into such a place. Christened Mary Jane Featherstone she was brought up by parents who were strict God-fearing Methodists. Her paternal grandparents were rich, but Polly's father's Wesleyan convictions were so strong that he refused his inheritance because the family fortune came from the sale of alcohol, and in his spare time he became a temperance lecturer.

The meeting of the paths of Polly and the plumber was the sequence of a series of events that would have bettered the plots of many of the Victorian melodramas staged there. Our young heroine was blessed with a good start in life; she was bright and her keen young mind enabled her to make the most of the good schooling she received. At seventeen years of age she was placed in a highly respected milliner's store to learn the art of trimming the large, ornate (and expensive) hats so favoured by Victorian ladies. But she found the work 'too pretty' – she had a zest for life and wanted to explore the world outside her sheltered upbringing. After one month she did the unthinkable: she ran away to Bradford.

Pretty Polly nearly got more than she bargained for. She was so naïve that she was on the point of booking accommodation in what could only be described as a place of ill repute. But young Polly was ignorant of such establishments and was probably seduced by the bright fashions and style of the young ladies living there. Fortunately for her, she was spotted by a travelling salesman who knew her and happened to be in the area on business. Tactfully, he shepherded her to a safe and respectable lodging house.

It was not long before she gained employment as a domestic help to a large family. In her free time she set out to explore this exciting, growing town for herself. One evening when in the town centre she heard trumpets, drums and so on sounding forth. She loved music and so was drawn to it. The source of the musical strains turned out to be a circle of happy young people in the market square. Fascinated she listened, watched and wondered. Who were these foolish folk? They were obviously religious, and Christians, because all their testimonies and songs were about Jesus. (In fact, they belonged to a group called the Christian Mission, destined to be renamed The Salvation Army a year later in 1878. William Booth, their leader, had visited Bradford in 1875.)

The meeting concluded with a ringing invitation to join them as they marched away to a nearby theatre where a great meeting was going to take place with gypsy Tillie Smith (the sister of gypsy Rodney Smith, whose powerful evangelistic preaching was attracting much favourable attention). Off they marched to the beat of the big drum and the blare of the trumpets and trombones; it was irresistible and Polly joined the following throng. Outside the big old theatre she hesitated; dare

she, a respectable middle-class Methodist, enter such a for-
bidden haunt? Checking to see that she was not observed by
any known acquaintances, she ducked inside the great doors,
and climbed up into a safe, secluded seat in the top gallery.

But there was no escaping the bright singing (the devil had
already lost some of his best tunes to them). The testimonies
were riveting and relevant; and when evangelist Tillie Smith
stood up to preach she did so with great conviction and a
directness Polly had never encountered from Methodist
pulpits, too many of which were settling down into cosy,
middle-class respectability.

Polly shifted uncomfortably in her seat, but there was no
wriggling away from the challenge. She found herself confronted with the claims of Christ in a way she had never
before experienced. It was personal and the cross of Christ
had never seemed so real; she realised that Christ had died for
her sins, and his precious blood was the only power that could
bring cleansing and forgiveness. When Tillie made an appeal
for salvation seekers to leave their seats and come to kneel at
the 'penitent form', Polly knew she had to respond. So down
she came, all the way from the top gallery to the front stalls,
where she knelt and earnestly sought the Saviour. After a time
Tillie came, knelt with her and led her to a saving knowledge
of the Lord Jesus. As she experienced the blessed assurance
that Jesus was now truly her Saviour she could contain herself
no longer and, jumping to her feet, threw her gloves up into
the air and shouted, 'Hallelujah; it is done!'

A few rows back, none of this was lost on a young plumber.
Already a deeply committed Christian, he had been praying
for all those who had responded to the appeal, but his heart
experienced more than a few flutters each time he caught a
glimpse of this attractive young lady. But when she stood up
and shouted it seemed to him that his heart missed a beat.
From that moment he had a feeling that there could be no
other girl for him.

The Industrial Revolution had roughly shunted little Bradford from the sleepy sidings onto the frenetic main line at the heart of Yorkshire's developing woollen industry. Bradford had been invaded by hungry hordes seeking work and wealth in the new, giant steam-driven mills. Tall mill chimneys belched out black smoke, fouling the atmosphere. But who cared? Yorkshire folk had a saying 'Where there's muck there's brass (money).'

Our eighteen-year-old plumber, a Yorkshireman through and through, had experienced more than his share of poverty. Born to John and Martha Wigglesworth in the village of Menston in 1859, he was christened Smith Wigglesworth in the local Anglican church. Times were hard and John Wigglesworth worked long hours for low pay. It was not easy providing for a wife, three sons and a daughter. He dug ditches, and pulled and cleaned turnips, and when Smith was six years old he helped to gather turnips. From morning till night he helped gather turnips until his little hands were sore. By the time he was seven, Smith was working in a woollen mill, along with his older brother, while his father also got work as a weaver. It was better than lifting turnips, but they had to rise at 5 a.m. and walk two miles to start work at 6 a.m. They worked a twelve-hour day, and it seemed never-ending to Smith.

His grandmother was an old-time Wesleyan Methodist. Smith loved going to the meetings with her and when he was eight years of age, at a time when God was powerfully present among them, Smith had an experience of salvation that was so real to him that he said in later life, 'I have never doubted my salvation since that day.'

Because of their poverty, Smith's schooling (then not compulsory) was neglected; but his spiritual education continued steadily. At twelve years of age he was confirmed in an Anglican church. When he was thirteen the family moved into Bradford (which had been a leading wool centre from the thirteenth century, but did not gain the status of a city until 1897) to be nearer the woollen mills, and life became easier for the Wigglesworths.

Smith had a great spiritual appetite and enjoyed making contact with the Plymouth Brethren. Their love of Bible study, and their emphasis on the second coming of Christ appealed to him. Smith was made a steam-fitter in the mill, and the man who taught him his new trade and his plumbing skills was a member of the Brethren, who also 'opened the word of God' to him during their meal breaks. He accepted the teaching about believer's baptism by immersion, and was so baptised when he was seventeen years old.

He was very much on fire for God and when William Booth's visit to Bradford in 1875 led to the formation of a new ministry, Smith was so impressed with their no-nonsense type of evangelism that he joined them. He participated enthusiastically in their nights of prayer, and in their soul-winning activities.

By the time he was eighteen years old he had become an experienced plumber and decided it was time to leave the mill. He was strong, and although uneducated and almost illiterate, he was bright, keen, of good personal appearance and ambitious. His own initiative got him a job with a leading plumber. He polished his shoes, put on a clean shirt, and went to the master plumber's home. He asked for a job, only to be told, 'No, I don't need anyone.' He hid his disappointment, replied politely, 'Thank you, sir. I'm sorry to have troubled you,' and turned to go. As the man watched him walk away, suddenly he had a change of heart. There was something different about this young man and he felt he could not let him go; and so, calling him back, he offered Smith a job.

His first assignment was fitting a row of houses with water piping. He completed the task in a week. When he returned, the boss said it was not possible to have finished it properly in that short time. But when he examined it he found it was excellent and could not fault it. In fact, Smith was such a fast worker that his new boss found it difficult to keep finding work for him.

Smith was enjoying his new life: he worked hard, prayed hard and played hard. He was a keen cyclist and his legs were so strong that others had great difficulty matching him riding up the hills. He inherited his love of nature – especially birds – from his father, and he also enjoyed cricket and bowls. He believed in keeping himself fit – physically, mentally and spiritually.

Polly's commitment to Christ proved to be real and lasting and she was soon making her mark. Smith's heart beat faster every time he saw her. As for Polly, in common with Smith's new boss, she soon realised that there was something very different about this young man. A friendship began to form between them, but Polly's outstanding abilities also impressed her leaders and they reported favourably on her to William Booth. He interviewed her and immediately recognised her potential, so much so that he offered to commission her as an officer without the usual training, and she accepted. She was proud to be an officer in The Salvation Army, even though it created a barrier to her growing friendship with Smith, because it was a strict rule that officers were only allowed to marry officers.

Soon Polly was posted to Leith, the port area adjoining Edinburgh in Scotland. Although there was no agreement between them, the thought of parting was hard for both of them and a test of their priorities. However, Polly threw herself wholeheartedly into her new appointment and soon proved the rightness of William Booth's decision to commission her. She was an excellent speaker, and quite fearless. The docks area of Leith was one of the toughest in its day. As she led her corps in their open-air meetings, local gangs regarded them as fair game and threw rotten eggs and tomatoes at Officer Polly Featherstone and her brave soldiers. A favourite ploy was to heat small coins and then throw them into the ring. They waited expectantly for curses as Polly or her soldiers burnt their fingers as they picked them up, but they were disappointed. Polly kept calm and continued the meeting, smiling, singing and testifying. Drink was a major problem and under its influence men behaved badly, inflicting more than one black eye on Polly in the course of her duties.

Not daunted she refused to be intimidated. The 'Army' taught its officers to care for the new converts, and Polly demonstrated her caring spirit. One convert was a young wife who lived on the sixth floor of a tenement building in a poor area of Leith. Her brute of a husband objected to her attending the meetings. When he returned home one day and found Polly praying with his wife, his anger boiled over and he threatened to throw Polly down the stairs if she did not stop praying immediately. Undeterred, Polly carried on praying. Incensed with rage he lifted her off her knees, threw her over his shoulder as though she were a sack of potatoes, and proceeded to carry her down the tenement stairs. His anger was further fuelled when he found that every step down the stairs was punctuated with Polly praying, 'Lord, save this man. Save his soul!' He fumed and raged but Polly prayed on. He had met his match, and by the time they reached the bottom step, he was the one who broke. In fact he was reduced to tears of repentance and that last step became a penitent form as Polly knelt beside him and led him to Christ.

This courageous spirit only added to her attractiveness, and it was no wonder that some of the men in her corps found their hearts beating faster. One young Scot in particular was really smitten and when it became known that Polly's time in Leith was due to end shortly, this soldier of the cross began to reveal his amorous intentions. It was brought to the attention of her senior officers and Polly was summoned before them and interrogated about the affair. When she vehemently denied any involvement, as a last resort they said, 'Polly, let's pray about it then.' But Polly was in first with her prayer:

Lord, you know that these men think I am interested in a Scotsman! Lord, you know that I am not; for if what these Scottish folk say about each other is true, they are all so stingy that they would nip a currant in two to save the other half. You know I don't believe that, Lord, for I have found them to be very kind; but you know, Lord, that I do not intend to marry anyone up here in Scotland.[1]

By the time she finished praying, her interrogators were more than ready to close the interview.

Polly had proved for herself that 'absence makes the heart grow fonder'; the period of separation had only served to confirm her warm feelings for Smith, the young plumber she had left in Bradford. In spite of the fact that Smith's lack of reading and writing skills severely limited communication between them (the telephone was only invented in 1876 and public phone boxes belonged to the future), the flame of love burned on in both their hearts. Around the same time that Polly was in Leith, Smith (then aged twenty years) took off for Liverpool, having heard that there were great opportunities in this large seaport which was then thriving commercially as never before. He was soon earning more money, but he did not become rich, except in faith. He was deeply moved at the appalling poverty that he encountered, especially round the docks area. Once again he attached himself to The Salvation Army (though he never actually joined). The terrible state of the many children in downtown Liverpool stirred him to action. He rented a shed at the dockside and each week he went round the slum areas inviting destitute and hungry boys

---

[1] S. H. Frodsham, *Smith Wigglesworth – Apostle of Faith* (Assemblies of God 1949), p. 10.

and girls to come for a good meal and to hear stories about Jesus. His employers supported him in this charitable enterprise but, even so, all his spare money went on food for the poor children. They came in droves, and he revelled in it, for God had given him a great heart of love for the poor, especially the children.

Although he was still hopeless at preaching or any form of public speaking, when it came down to one to one, he was in his element; he excelled in personal soul-winning – a gift God had given him when only a boy. He loved talking to individuals about his Saviour and as he visited the hospitals and ships he had the joy of leading many to place their trust in Jesus as Saviour and Lord. In his few years in Liverpool he matured significantly.

But in 1882, aged twenty-three, he felt the pull of his Yorkshire roots and returned to Bradford with the ambition to open his own plumbing business, and devote all his spare time to evangelism. He succeeded in this bold venture, as he had got his priorities right. Although he was still virtually illiterate he had a genuine talent for business and, above all, God was with him. All the time he was in Liverpool his heart could never forget Polly; and he prayed that God would keep her for him. He knew that there could never be any other girl for him. He need not have worried for Polly knew that Smith was the only man for her. She returned to Bradford and shortly afterwards resigned her commission in The Salvation Army, though she remained a fervent supporter of General William Booth and his work to the end of her days. Nevertheless, she joined a new evangelistic group known as Elizabeth Baxter's Blue Ribbon Army, which had established itself in Bradford. Although similar to The Salvation Army, the differences appealed to her.

Once Smith and Polly were back in Bradford it was not long before they met up again. Each knew and believed that, in God's loving providence, he had brought them together. It was a love match and none of their friends was surprised to hear that they planned to marry before the end of 1882. Five eventful and character-forming years had passed since their paths first crossed on the night of Polly's conversion. On their wedding day, Polly was twenty-two years old, and Smith a year older. It was a union made in heaven, but the path of true love does not run smoothly all the time.

They were both deeply in love with each other and with Christ. They built their home and family on Christian principles; children were joyously accepted as God's gift, and over the years they were blessed with a daughter, Alice, and four sons, Seth, Harold, Ernest and George. They prayed for their children before they were born, that they would belong to the Lord. Smith happily carried their children to the meetings, as well as looking after them while Polly preached. Their new home, 70 Victor Road, Bradford, though they little knew it, was destined to become world famous.

Smith's plumbing business prospered, and so did Polly's preaching; she was a gifted speaker and soul-winner and much sought after. Remarkably for those Victorian times, Smith encouraged her to continue her gifted ministry of evangelism, while he concentrated on building up his new plumbing business.

One of the first things Polly did was to take on the task of teaching Smith to read and write. This she undertook gladly, and Smith applied himself – realising its importance. He frequently expressed his gratitude for her patience and skill, and said, 'She taught me to read properly and to write – though unfortunately she never succeeded in teaching me to spell!' However, it was not easy for either of them, and was an early test of their love, the more so because male chauvinism remained the order of the day in Victorian society and in church life.

His new business enterprise prospered and as the name of Wigglesworth became known for good plumbing work he was soon travelling to all parts of Bradford. He discovered many needy areas without any churches in them; he shared this with Polly and they prayerfully searched out and rented a suitable building to start a mission in one such area. Once found they quickly made it ready – but that was the easy part. Smith, though a great personal worker, still could never preach without breaking down and weeping, whereas Polly had become an experienced and successful evangelist, with a good singing voice. The arrangement was agreed that she should lead the meetings and preach, while Smith sat by her on the platform. When she invited seekers to come forward, he would go to the penitent form to pray with them and lead them to trust in the Saviour. In his words, 'Polly's work was to put down the net – and mine was to land the fish.' It worked extremely well and they made a great team. The mission, like the plumbing business, did well.

Their marriage and family was also doing well. They had five children and for several years were very happy: Smith made a good father, Polly a wonderful mother; they prayed about everything and to all intents and purposes had no real problems. Smith frequently looked after the children so that Polly could fulfil her many speaking engagements; she was in demand outside the mission as well as popular in it.

Smith too was in great demand; he had gained a reputation for being honest and doing good work, and he was becoming quite prosperous. He thrived on hard work and grew busier and busier; but although he continued to prosper materially, his spirituality began to decline. An exceptionally cold winter aggravated the situation to breaking point. The freezing weather meant frozen and burst pipes and more work, with better pay for plumbers. He had less and less time for God and for his family, his heart becoming as cold and hard as the frozen pipes he was mending. The big freeze did so much damage that the plumbers' bonanza lasted two years. But these were terribly testing times for Polly: when Smith got home after working overtime, day after day, he was tired, bad-tempered and difficult to live with.

Somehow, throughout Smith's two-year spiritual winter, Polly steadfastly refused to degenerate into a nagging wife; instead, she did her utmost to deepen her devotion to Christ, and patiently to lift Smith out of his black hole. She had every right to feel aggrieved because she too was on perpetual overtime, having to do virtually everything at the mission, on top of the housework and cooking and caring for Smith and the five children, and honouring her many outside preaching engagements, not to mention the number of guests they freely entertained. One night, however, things came to a head when she arrived home later than expected after being out preaching. As soon as she set foot in the house, he raised his strong voice angrily: 'I am the master of this house, and I am not going to have you coming home as late as this.' Instead of shouting back at him, Polly quietly but firmly responded, 'I know you are my husband, but Christ is my Master.' This further incensed him and in a fury he pushed her out of the house through the back door and locked her out. What a predicament, but he had overlooked two things in this bad-tempered tactic. First, he had not locked the front door; second, he should have known Polly better than to think that she would capitulate so easily. While he fumed inside the house, Polly on the outside went round to the front door, found it unlocked and entered – laughing her head off. At first Smith stared, uncertain what to do next, but as she stood there laughing and laughing and treating it all as a huge joke, he could not help himself – and he started to laugh along with her. The worst of the crisis was over, but she still needed to persist in her wise and patient attitude until he was his true self again. Throughout it all, she somehow managed to hold on to her priceless sense of humour.

It was a wonderful day for both of them when, in their own

home on Victor Road, he knelt and renewed his consecration to Christ. In his later years he confessed to trusted friends:

> I can remember when I used to go white with rage and shake all over with temper. I could hardly hold myself together. I waited on God for ten days, and in those ten days I was being emptied out and the life of the Lord Jesus was being wrought in me. My wife testified of the transformation.[2]

Polly said, 'I never saw such a change. For example, with his meals, whatever I cook for him now, everything is just right.'

His plumbing business continued to prosper but now it no longer controlled him. He was fully restored and on fire for God. Once again he was pulling his weight at the mission, though it was still Polly who was doing the preaching.

Smith got his plumbing supplies weekly from Leeds, about ten miles away. During one visit he met a group who had started divine healing meetings there. He was very interested and after carefully comparing their teaching with the Bible he was convinced, and started taking sick people with him. However, he kept this from Polly at first, fearing that she might not approve. But it was impossible to keep anything secret from her for long: she knew him too well! To his relief and surprise she also felt it was right. In fact, she not only accompanied him to the meetings, but asked for prayer for herself for a particular problem. She was immediately healed and it was not long before both of them were praying for the sick as a regular part of their ministry of the gospel.

Together they entered into a pledge that they would trust the Lord to be their Healer, with no drugs and no doctors. However, when Smith was taken very ill (subsequently diagnosed with appendicitis) he told Polly to call the doctor – to cover her from any blame, should it prove to be fatal. In fact,

---

[2] Jack Hywel-Davies, *Baptised by Fire* (Hodder 1987), p. 44.

he experienced a wonderful healing, which confounded the doctor who had given up hope.

Smith and Polly were regular visitors to the Keswick Convention in the Lake District. The rich expository ministry of well-known international speakers was a delight to them and they both embraced Keswick's teaching on 'the Second Blessing' and sanctification. They were hungry for all that God had for them, and his blessing clearly rested upon their family, the plumbing business, and the Mission. The latter prospered to such an extent that they had to find a larger building and the Mission was moved to Bowland Street. But Polly was still the preacher; Smith, though mighty in prayer and personal work, was hopeless at platform ministry.

Smith's transformation came in 1907, when he went to Sunderland to sound out for himself the outpouring of the Holy Spirit. This was reported to be happening at the Anglican church in Monkwearmouth under the godly vicar, Revd A.A. Boddy, and in conjunction with the visit of Revd T.B. Barratt from Norway. The phenomenon capturing the newspaper headlines was the speaking in other tongues as on the Day of Pentecost (Acts 2:4), claimed as evidence of the baptism of the Holy Spirit. At the end of his four-day visit, Smith experienced a mighty infilling of God's Spirit accompanied by speaking in tongues. He sent a telegram to Polly with the glad news 'Have received the Baptism in the Holy Spirit and have spoken in tongues.'

Polly was sceptical, and when he arrived home she looked him up and down and snorted, 'So, you've been speaking in tongues?' 'Yes,' he replied. 'Well,' she retorted, 'I'd have you know I am as baptised as you are and I don't speak with tongues. I've been preaching for twenty years while you have sat there "tongue-tied" – so, on Sunday, you'll preach and I'll be there to see it.' And with a toss of her still-pretty head, she left Smith standing there, deflated and dismayed.

On Sunday morning everyone at the Mission was soon

aware of the Smith–Polly rift, because for the first time Polly was not on the platform but sitting on the back row with Florence, a close friend. Even as Smith walked to the vacant platform he was without a message, but then it was given to him and out it poured like a fast-flowing river: 'The Spirit of the Lord is upon me' was his text from Isaiah 61. He began to preach with a power and fluency that astounded Polly! She could not believe it. 'That's not my Smith,' she muttered to herself. As he continued she was so taken aback that she shifted uncomfortably along the length of the bench, saying, 'That's not my Smith. What's happened to the man?' Afterwards she confessed, 'It was a remarkable event'; which finished with many declaring, 'We want what you've got.' And they received it. It was not long before Polly also sought and received the baptism of the Holy Spirit with speaking in tongues. It marked the beginning of a remarkable partnership in preaching in which they shared the pulpit. Sadly, though, it was not destined to last long.

One of their most successful missions outside Bradford was in Shropshire; God used their dual ministry in a remarkable way in what many recognised as a breath of true revival. Back in Bradford they had a tall flagpole erected outside the Mission and a large flag made bearing the message in bold letters on one side 'Christ died for our sins'; on the other side 'I am the Lord that healeth thee'. Another joint venture also blessed in a remarkable way was a 'Banquet for the Poor'. The words of Jesus in Luke 14:13–14, 'But when you give a banquet, invite the poor, the crippled, the lame, the blind, and you will be blessed . . .' were quickened to Smith one day as he was reading his Bible. He shared this with Polly and the project was launched. They put on a splendid banquet and invited all the poor and sick to come – without charge. They came in droves and were welcomed and feasted as though they were royalty. Impressive, up-to-date testimonies by people who had been healed followed the feast. They then prayed for all the sick who wanted prayer, and many outstanding miracles of healing took place. God honoured their obedience and faith. It was a night to be remembered.

It was not long before Smith knew that the time had come for him to leave his plumbing business and concentrate on the ministry God had given him. Invitations to speak were pouring in and the plumbing was getting neglected. However, he and Polly still had family commitments and it required a big step of faith to relinquish a prosperous business. Polly agreed with Smith that it was the right time and the right thing to do; it was not easy, but God helped them to meet every commitment.

Their love for Christ and their love for each other matured and increased over the years, every trial and difficulty making that love stronger and deeper. Then, in 1913, when they were both over fifty years of age, death, the only power that could part them, paid an unexpected visit. Polly was a thrilling preacher and frequently she got so taken up with her message that heaven seemed nearer to her than earth. In fact, she lovingly and half laughingly once confided to Smith, 'You watch me when I'm preaching – sometimes I seem to get so near to heaven that one day I'll be off.' And that's just what happened. Smith was due to preach in Glasgow, while Polly was to preach at the Mission; his train was due to leave later and so she had said her goodbye as she left the house. The time came for Smith to leave home for the railway station, but just as he was about to leave the house a policeman and a doctor confronted him. One look at their faces told him that something was wrong. Gravely they informed him of what had happened. After Polly had finished preaching she had collapsed and died at the Mission.

The news spread quickly and soon the house was filled with stunned sympathisers. Polly's lifeless body was carried into the house. The doctor told Smith, 'She is dead, and we can do no more for her.' Smith looked down at the prostrate form of his beloved Polly; it was so hard to take in that this was the vivacious wife who had left the house only a few short hours before. His heart was deeply moved and with that audacious faith that was to become the hallmark of his future worldwide ministry, he stood beside her corpse and commanded death to give her up. In his own words he described later to friends what happened: 'She came back to me for a moment. Then God said to me: "She is mine; her work is done," – and I knew what He meant.'

He was spared to live another thirty-four years, but also died unexpectedly, in 1947, at the funeral of one of his closest friends. He never forgot his dear Polly and how much he owed to her. More than once he expressed his debt of love to her as follows: 'All that I am today, I owe under God, to my precious wife. She was lovely. She became a great help to me in my spiritual life. She was an inspiration to holiness.'

# 5
## *Billy and Ruth Graham*

It came to pass that a certain young student was climbing the college steps when a human whirlwind swept past her. He was going so fast that all she saw was a tall blur. 'Wow – there goes a young man in a hurry,' she thought, little realising how right she was.

A few days later at one of the Sunday morning prayer meetings (this was Wheaton, one of America's top Christian accredited colleges of liberal arts) she heard a new voice raised in prayer. It was strong, clear and with a note of urgent authority. 'Now there is a man who knows how to address the Almighty,' she thought, and was impressed, for she was a deeply spiritual and prayerful person.

Once the prayer meeting had ended she felt free to open her eyes and look around at the students as they dispersed to their various team assignments. The 'passing blur and the praying voice of power' suddenly came into focus, and she realised that they were one and the same, new student William Franklin Graham who had been transferred from Florida Bible College. Young as he was he had already gained a reputation as a promising preacher on whom God's hand was resting. Like Saul of old 'he could not be hid' – at six feet two inches he stood out in the crowd of students. Also, in common with Old Testament King Saul, he came from farming stock – his lean, manly face spoke of fresh air and a zest for life and attracted not a few interested glances. Billy, however, initially found Wheaton College and nearby Chicago to be rather out of his league. Dresswise he felt like a hick and missed Florida Bible College and his many friends there.

Over the next four weeks the young lady student learned more about Billy, who was already making his presence felt and heard on the college campus. The college grapevine soon provided its own condensed CV of this lively – if still somewhat raw – new character. He was born four days before the end of World War II, on 7th November 1918; his father was a dairy farmer in Charlotte, North Carolina. As a lively teenager Billy attended a Presbyterian church with his parents, but had no real interest in religion at that stage. An eleven-week crusade in Charlotte by the renowned but controversial evangelist Dr Mordecai Ham in 1934 changed all that. Billy's parents joined the great crowds of up to five thousand who flocked to hear him and along with many more were helped into a deeper Christian experience. Although Billy, then almost sixteen years old, at first refused to attend Dr Ham's meetings, after several weeks his curiosity got the better of him. He continued to attend and came under conviction, finally responding openly to the evangelist's appeal. His conversion proved genuine and his new-found enthusiasm provoked one teacher into making fun of him in front of the class when she labelled him 'Preacher Graham'.

Graduating from Sharon High School in 1936, to save money for college Billy spent the summer as a door-to-door salesman for Fuller Bush Company. He enrolled in Bob Jones College but, finding it 'over-restrictive', switched to Florida Bible College where he quickly settled down and enjoyed his years there (1937–40). Although inexperienced he was already proving himself an effective preacher with a definite evangelistic gift. He was persuaded to be baptised by immersion and was approved for ordination as a Southern Baptist minister; then he was appointed assistant pastor to a Dr Minder. After graduating, his pursuit of further education led him to Wheaton in September 1940.

It was in his first term that Billy made friends with a young man called John, who had served in the Navy and was working his way through college by using a small truck to move items for people – including furniture. Billy was willingly recruited into his little business, welcoming the extra money. John felt God was calling him to the mission field, possibly China. In the course of conversation he described in glowing terms a girl student in one of the junior classes as being one of the most beautiful and dedicated Christian girls he had ever met. It just so happened that this vision of perfection had been born and brought up in China, the daughter of Presbyterian missionaries Dr and Mrs D. Nelson Bell. Her father was a medical doctor.

Some days after their conversation, when Billy and John were dirty and sweaty from hauling furniture around on the truck, the young lady walked down the street where they were working – not surprising, as it was near to the women's hall of residence.

As soon as John spotted her he became visibly excited and blurted out, 'Billy – look, here comes the girl I told you about.' Billy looked up, stretched to his full six feet two inches, and found himself gazing down at a beautiful girl. She looked so stunning that she could have walked out of a Hollywood film set. When Billy realised that her hazel eyes were fastened upon him, he felt embarrassed, suddenly conscious of his grimy, sweaty appearance. He now understood why John was so smitten by her, and found himself affected likewise. When John introduced them Billy was so flustered that he could only stammer out a few polite words of response.

He was so overwhelmed by her that it took him a full month before he plucked up enough courage to ask her for a date. He never imagined he had any chance of getting a date with a girl of her calibre, especially when he learned that she dedicated her Saturday nights to prayer and study of God's word in preparation for the Lord's day. He wondered what kind of romance a college student could have with a person so deeply spiritual and so physically beautiful. She was refined, witty, talented, and from a very gifted family. He was just a farmer's boy from Carolina, who was struggling to improve his poor grades. Apart from that he was older than most of the other students – the only outstanding thing about him was that he owned a car, an old one at that.

As for Ruth Bell, she found herself pleased to make, at last, the personal acquaintance of the 'young man in a hurry with the praying voice of power'. She sensed that inside that raw, unpolished exterior there was a character of unusual potential. Consequently, near Christmas when Billy plucked up courage to invite her to accompany him on a Sunday afternoon to hear Handel's *Messiah*, she accepted – to his surprise and delight.

In his pre-conversion days Billy had enjoyed friendships with a number of girls, but riding up and down the main street of his home town with a girl in his old jalopy was very different to sitting and listening to *The Messiah*. Yet he found his heart had never beat faster than when sitting next to Ruth Bell. Afterwards, as they walked together and sat down to talk together over a cup of coffee, he found it hard to believe that anyone could be so spiritual yet beautiful at the same time; but he knew that in Ruth Bell he had found such a rare treasure. As usual, he was in a hurry and wanted to push ahead with his new-found love to such an extent that his close friends had to caution him against going too fast.

In fact, they would have been even more surprised had they been able to follow Ruth Bell to her room that night. After sitting through the *Messiah* concert Ruth already felt in her heart that Billy was the man for her. Ruth knelt and told the

Lord that if she could spend the rest of her life serving him with Billy, she would consider it the greatest privilege imaginable.

Ruth had a strong feeling in her heart that God had brought them together. It so happened that she was not the only one who thought that. One of Ruth's teachers at Wheaton was Miss Edith Torrey, the daughter of the outstanding evangelist and Bible teacher, Dr Reuben A. Torrey. She was a true daughter of her gifted father and, according to Ruth, taught the Bible with a thoroughness that the students found almost frightening. Although she may have been lacking in charm, behind her spectacles were discerning and caring eyes, and inside her tall, bony frame beat a heart of gold, with a deep love and concern for the well-being of her students. Miss Torrey soon had a strong conviction that Ruth and the new student, Billy Graham, were made for each other. It was only after Ruth and Billy were engaged that she shared her secret with them: she had been praying for months that the two of them would come together!

Edith Torrey felt a special closeness to Ruth who, after spending the first seventeen years of her life on the mission field in China, had come to Wheaton, having had to leave her parents behind. Ruth was so physically beautiful that it was obvious from the first day that she was going to turn the heads of all the male students. But Miss Torrey's fears for Ruth evaporated when she discovered that her beauty was more than skin deep: she had an inner beauty as a deeply spiritual person and a fully committed believer.

The more she discovered about Ruth's background the more certain she became that this girl was not going to be swept off her feet by any man. God's hand was upon Ruth Bell and she would surely become a very special woman in the purposes of God. Miss Torrey discovered that inside that petite and pretty exterior was a strong character that had been steeled in the furnace of missionary life. As a medical missionary, her father Dr Nelson Bell was constantly called to practise his surgical skills in extremely dangerous and horrific circumstances. Life in the eastern Chinese province of Northern Kiangsu provided more than enough excitement: nature produced monsoons and sandstorms of frightening ferocity; there was constant unrest due to the dangers and insecurities of civil war; ruthless bandits preyed on the people; not to mention epidemics that were swifter and more murderous than any swords or guns wielded by the military and bandits.

But with her parents and their missionary colleagues Ruth grew up surrounded by a faith and a love that refused to bend to any threats or dangers. More than one brave missionary was lying in a martyr's grave in China. One such, whom Ruth had known as Uncle Jack, had been captured by bandits and shot in cold blood.

In spite of all that, Ruth's childhood years were still mostly happy and full of love in her home in the hospital compound. Her father devoted his healing skills to all who needed them in the name of Christ. Not that it was ever easy, or long lasting. On one occasion in the local jail Dr Bell treated a captured bandit with a severe head wound. He cleaned the wound, and stitched and bandaged it with the same care that he gave to all his patients. But only a few hours later as her father passed the city gate he saw that same bandaged but now severed head hanging over the gate – the bandit had been executed.

At the age of thirteen Ruth was faced with the prospect of having to leave home for boarding school. It was all too much for her and she spent the last night praying to die before morning! If it was agony for Ruth, it was equally painful for her loving parents. It was yet another sacrifice that missionaries with young families were called to make. The parents wanted the best for their children and in this case the best available was the Foreign School in Pyeng Yang, North Korea. In 1933 the distance was measured not so much in miles as in days: the school was about seven days' journey away by river and sea. Korea, although then not divided, was under Japanese occupation as it had been since 1910. There were five children in that party bound for Pyeng Yang, including Ruth's older sister, Rosa, who had already spent one year there and was enjoying it. But Ruth was of a different disposition and during the first few weeks cried herself to sleep every night. However, in later life she came to understand the value of those tough times and was grateful for her training and trials.

Four years later she was ready for college, which meant returning to America. Her departure was rudely interrupted and delayed when Shanghai fell to the invading Japanese armies in August 1937. The American consul urged the missionaries to go north to Haichow, where an American Navy destroyer would be waiting to evacuate them. Dr and Mrs Bell, along with other missionaries, made the journey safely and the destroyer took them to the port of Tsingtao. Dr Bell eventually managed to secure a place for Ruth on a troopship that was evacuating naval families from the war zone. They stayed on in China as long as possible, but eventually they too had to return to America. At seventeen Ruth was maturer and better able to cope with the trauma of leaving her parents and dealing with the excitement of leaving the land of her birth for Wheaton College near Chicago.

There were no tears on her pillow at Wheaton; she felt at home immediately. Even so, growing up in China, while giving her a rare experience of life on the other side of the world, had also left her rather naïve when it came to dealing with life in the increasingly sophisticated Western world. Fortunately, she was a quick learner who soon learned to adjust to life in her new environment. As she was the most stunning girl on campus, Billy was not the first man she dated, but he was the last and she knew in her heart of hearts that he was the one for her.

With Billy it was love at first sight and after that first date at the *Messiah* concert he felt certain that he was the man Ruth would marry. Over the months that followed, Billy and Ruth had many long and earnest discussions about their respective futures. She set about persuading Billy that he too should consider going to Tibet as a missionary. Billy was now much more certain about his own future. He was sure that God had called him to preach the gospel of Christ. Very soon he was sure of something else: Ruth was a determined young lady.

Some months passed and Ruth's fixation on Tibet remained. Billy, though, with a higher wisdom decided to let God do his courting for him. He endeavoured not to pressure her, but he did not stifle all his persuasive powers – to do so would have been tantamount to a denial of his true self and of his growing love and respect for her. Their devout discussions continued and covered their relationship as well as Tibet. They did not really argue but neither did they see eye to eye. Both of them had strong wills, but their love and mutual respect was enabling them to make adjustments and allowances. During this time they were finding out a great deal about each other.

Even so, Billy had low moments when he despaired of ever winning Ruth: he felt that culturally she was superior to him. He was only a farmer's boy, whereas she was a doctor's daughter. Her upbringing in China seemed to have given her a wider understanding of the world at large, in contrast to his limited world circumscribed by a dairy farm in the back-of-beyond in Carolina.

Another key difference between them was their denominational allegiances: Billy was Baptist, Ruth Presbyterian. The issue of believer's baptism by immersion gave rise to some lively discussions, but did not lead to a settlement. The one thing that they agreed upon was that they were both strong willed. Ruth realised that Billy had a mind of his own. She also knew in her heart of hearts that she would not want him any other way. Equally, Billy was convinced that Ruth was the most determined girl he had ever met. He loved her more than ever and would not have her be any different, except perhaps on two things: Tibet and baptism. Although at times she exasperated him – especially when she proved his equal in their heated discussions – he knew that he loved her and would find it hard to live without her. Another determining factor for him was that she reminded him so much of his own beloved mother.

At last he was confident enough, in spite of their unresolved differences, to propose marriage; but instead of responding immediately she kept him waiting for her answer – and still had the temerity to express her desire that he should keep an open mind about Tibet, even though she was aware under-neath that Billy did not feel called to be a missionary.

The day finally dawned when the evangelist in him rose up and he determined to make his appeal for a definite decision. Point-blank he asked Ruth, 'Do you believe that God brought us together?' On that point she readily agreed – she had no doubt that God had brought them together. 'In that case', Billy said, 'God will lead me, and you will do the following.'

Even though Ruth did not say yes right there on the spot, Billy knew in his heart that she was seriously considering his proposal. Before she had time to deliver a considered response her older sister Rosa became very ill. The diagnosis was tuberculosis and Rosa was placed in a hospital many miles away in New Mexico. Ruth left Wheaton to be with her, and Billy was kept waiting almost two years for the answer he wanted. It was a testing period for both of them to be apart for so long. They kept in touch by letter and the absence deep-ened the feelings between them.

Billy was preaching in Florida when a letter arrived from Ruth postmarked 6th July 1941. He tore it open and when he read in one of the first sentences the magic words 'I'll marry you' he was beside himself with joy. In bed that night he read that letter over and over again. At the first opportunity he raced off to buy an engagement ring. When at last they were able to meet on Ruth's return from New Mexico, under a rising moon Billy presented her with his ring and for the very first time he kissed Ruth on the lips. He thought it was so romantic, but later Ruth informed him that she thought he was going to swallow her!

Ruth accepted the ring, but with a gesture that reveals much about her character and the love with which she honoured her parents she told Billy, apologetically, that she could not wear it until she had their permission. As a letter would have been too slow, she sent a telegram, to which her parents replied immediately with an emphatic and happy yes.

Later that summer Billy went to meet Ruth's parents for the first time. When she rushed out of the house to greet him, expecting a hug and a kiss, he was so nervous at the prospect of meeting her distinguished parents that he froze. It was not long, however, before his tenseness melted away in the loving atmosphere of the Bells' home. Soon he realised that in Ruth God had given him not only the woman of his dreams but the most wonderful in-laws as well, and he knew they were going to enrich his life immeasurably.

The young engaged couple were still studying at Wheaton College. In spite of being busy (especially Billy who, in addition to his studies was preaching regularly and still moving furniture with his friend John) their relationship deepened over that year. However, the course of true love is seldom smooth and to Billy's consternation he found that the issue of Tibet, and his uncertainty in that direction, led Ruth to share her feeling that they should stop dating and not see each other for a while. Billy's decisiveness came to the rescue again. In that case, he dared to suggest that he would appreciate it if she returned the ring. It was exactly what Ruth needed to get her thinking straight once and for all. That ring meant a great deal to her and she had no intention of returning it; so it was settled at last. Ruth lost her lingering doubt and kept the ring on her finger.

World-changing events in the Far East eventually confirmed the rightness of the outcome of the ring episode. Within a few years the door to Tibet was closed to missionaries and Ruth realised that if she had insisted on having her way, at most she would have been able to spend only four years in Tibet – and (in her own words) 'I would have missed the opportunity of a lifetime serving God with the finest man I know.'[1] Nevertheless, she never regretted that longing to go to Tibet; she believes that God was 'testing her willingness while at the same time preparing her for many long separations'[2] which lay ahead as the wife of the man who was destined to be one of the most successful evangelists of the twentieth century.

Ruth kept her ring and they both kept their heads: they did not rush ahead with their marriage plans, but agreed that they should first complete their graduation courses. In January 1943, halfway through their final year, Billy was invited to the pastorate of Western Springs Baptist Church, twenty miles from Wheaton and near to the University of Chicago, which would be convenient if he decided to do advanced studies. Conscious of his forthcoming marriage and the responsibility of supporting Ruth, Billy accepted the pastorate. But he forgot to consult Ruth and she was not pleased when he informed her of what he had done without talking it over with her.

They both graduated in June 1943 and were married in August in Montreat, North Carolina. Their brief honeymoon over, they went to Western Springs where they were warmly welcomed as the new pastor and his wife by the Baptist church, which had less than a hundred members. Within a

---

[1] Ruth Bell Graham, *It's My Turn* (Hodder 1983), p. 53.
[2] *Ibid.*

few days Ruth was taken ill. Billy cared for her and did the cooking, mainly for himself, as Ruth had no appetite. Her temperature continued to rise and she was admitted to hospital. Billy was due to preach in Ohio and by the time he returned home Ruth had been discharged from hospital and had tidied their apartment home. The two young lovebirds quickly settled into married life.

A sense of humour is a great help in married life, but Ruth's mischievous brand of humour was not always appreciated. For example, some ten weeks into their marriage Ruth put a PS on the bottom of a card home to her parents informing them of 'an addition to the family'. Her parents assumed it meant she was pregnant and immediately despatched a letter with their warm congratulations! In fact, the addition was nothing more than an alley cat, which they had adopted and given the name Junior. Billy was not amused and Ruth had a lot of apologising to do to her parents as well as to him.

College life was over and now they were settling in to their first pastorate and adjusting to married life. The church soon began to grow under their leadership and Billy's inspiring and challenging preaching. It was not long before Billy was preaching on WCFL in Chicago, a radio station that covered areas in the midwest and south and east. It made life hectic for both of them.

On top of his many commitments, Billy also became very involved with the burgeoning Youth for Christ movement. His God-given gift as an evangelist was soon evident in the many who responded to his appeal to commit their lives to Christ as Saviour and Lord. Ruth knew in her heart that this was surely his God-given calling and not only backed him totally, but also spoke out strongly against anything that might interfere with it. She also accepted that as an evangelist he would be away from home a great deal.

In 1944 it was Billy's turn to be ill – with mumps. Mumps in adults is often regarded as a cause for laughter, but as a twenty-six-year-old male he did not find his illness humorous. Even Ruth, as a doctor's daughter, found his swollen glands a tempting source of amusement – and, it seems, so did everyone she phoned to tell the news that Billy had mumps. However, she knew that it could prove serious and nursed him lovingly. He became worse with a raging fever and mumps developed into orchitis. This laid him low for two months and the specialist fought to save Billy's life. Many people prayed and God heard the prayers. Billy and Ruth were able to go away together as he convalesced, but the doctor warned that the orchitis could possibly have rendered Billy infertile – a serious blow as they both loved children. It was months before Billy fully recovered but the enforced period of rest gave them the opportunity for a quieter life with more time together. They came to know each other better and to appreciate each other even more. Their love for each other, and their mutual understanding, strengthened and deepened. It gave them breathing space to lay a solid foundation for their union before being caught up in the whirlwind life into which they were about to be launched.

His successful engagements with the growing Youth for Christ movement led to his being invited to become their full-time national and international organiser. Billy and Ruth discussed this for weeks, as well as praying, and finally agreed that Billy should accept the post. It was a major step forward. He resigned his pastorate and between 1945 and 1947, in that crucial period for the world following World War II, he was preaching in Britain and Europe as well as all over the USA and Canada. As he was boarding a train for yet another rally, this time in Indianapolis, he was handed a telegram from Ruth with the marvellous news that she was pregnant! Their joy knew no bounds – especially in view of the doctor's warning that Billy's illness had possibly rendered him unable to father a child. Ruth told Billy that in view of his constant travelling she did not wish to be left in Chicago alone. Should they not consider asking her parents if they could accommodate them in their home in Montreat, North Carolina, until the baby was born? Billy saw the wisdom of this and Dr and Mrs Bell readily agreed to the arrangement. In the early months of her pregnancy it was possible for Ruth to be with Billy on many of his preaching tours. Everywhere they went Ruth noticed that Billy had developed a new interest in babies; it was a happy time for both of them.

On 21st September 1945 Ruth gave birth to their first child, Virginia Leftwich Graham, always affectionately referred to as Gigi. It eased matters greatly that Ruth was with her parents, and from time to time she was able to leave Gigi in their care while she accompanied Billy. The young couple loved every precious moment they could spend together, but Ruth now found herself pulled in two directions. She and Billy realised that her motherhood was going to have to take precedence. They accepted that Billy's God-given ministry of an evangelist was going to call for the constant sacrifice of each other's company, but the pain of a seemingly endless stream of goodbyes did not lessen with the passing years. Ruth's support for her husband was total, as was her commitment to being the best mother possible. As for Billy, Ruth was the love of his life and his devotion to her continued to deepen over the years.

In 1946, with the Youth for Christ team, he spent his first preaching tour in Europe. He returned to Britain in 1947 and Ruth was able to join him for part of the time, but she was longing to get back to little Gigi and so flew back to the US two months before the end of Billy's tour. Billy missed Ruth desperately and was grateful for her regular, loving letters. Just when Billy was beginning to feel guilty about his repeated absences, a letter from Ruth was like soothing oil to his anxious heart. She wrote, 'I feel closer to you than ever before. . . . Wherever you are, I go with you in mind and heart – praying for you continually.' Billy knew that God had given him a treasure of a wife in whom he could trust (see Proverbs 31:11).

The year 1948 was eventful for both of them: Ruth gave birth to a second daughter, Anne Morrow, and Billy was invited to become President of North-Western Schools, following the death of its founder, Dr W.B. Riley. Ruth selflessly and firmly counselled Billy that he was called by God to be an evangelist not an educator. After much prayer and thought Billy said he was only willing to take it on as interim president, a position he occupied with considerable success for four years, in spite of the many other claims made upon him. This included family responsibilities with the birth of a third daughter, Ruth Bell, at the end of 1950. In 1952, however, he finally persuaded the directors of North-Western to accept his resignation (his first attempt had been refused). Set free from that heavy commitment, almost immediately he started the Billy Graham Evangelistic Association. He had learned much as the youngest college president in the nation, but it was a huge relief to be totally free to concentrate on being an evangelist. While he was still college president the historic crusade in Los Angeles took place in 1949, the success of which made him a national figure with a stature to be reckoned with. The two-week crusade lasted for eight glorious weeks, by the end of which Billy was physically exhausted. Invitations poured in and expectations of him were sky-high; but Billy knew that the success was God's doing, and gave him all the glory. He knew that he was still just a country preacher with too much on his plate, and had a real fear that he would be unable to live up to the awesome responsibility that had been thrust upon him.

Living history confirms that Billy and Ruth handled their growing fame with unfailing humility, integrity and wisdom. The Billy Graham Evangelistic Association went from strength to strength, the fine team he built around him sharing the burden and the vision that grew to incorporate evangelistic films, national radio and TV programmes, and the magazines *Christianity Today* and *Decision*. Soon Billy was an international celebrity and certainly the best-known evangelist in the world in the second half of the twentieth century.

His visit to the allied troops fighting in the Korean War in 1953 strengthened his bond with General Eisenhower, who had been elected as US President in 1952. Billy and Ruth have found themselves as guests at the White House on many occasions. Their love and faithfulness to each other has never wavered and neither has their devotion and commitment to their God-given calling ever been called into question.

There are many highlights in Billy's crusades, such as London Harringay in 1954; Tell Scotland in 1955; New York in 1957; but these were only the beginning of a growing stream of international crusades and seemingly endless successes – including India, the Philippines, Hong Kong, Formosa (Taiwan), Japan, Australia, Africa, the Middle East, South America, Mexico, Moscow, Poland, Yugoslavia, China, North Korea, Ireland, South Africa.

Life has been costly for the Grahams, not only in terms of physical strength and spiritual integrity, but also in the tremendous sacrifice of precious time with each other and their children. Ruth's secret has been in her commitment to the marriage vows made before God, and to seeking first his kingdom. 'In sickness and in health, for better for worse, for richer for poorer' – they have both been true to their marriage vows. They have honoured God and his word and the gospel of Christ above all; and they have both honoured each other and held their love as a most sacred and precious thing.

# 6

## *Jacob and Rachel*

The two little boys sat up in their beds ready for a story from their lovely mother, Rebekah. They were twins, but no one would have guessed it from looking at them. And their home was a tent, but few would have realised that from their bedroom, which was large, richly furnished and adorned with colourful hangings of finest wool. The older one had striking red hair, and appeared to have hair on much of his body too – unusual for his age, but promising outstanding physical strength and agility. The younger had a head of shiny black hair like his mother's, but with soft, smooth skin on his face and body. They were excited because tonight she had promised to tell them how she came to meet and marry their father.

She had their attention immediately when she said that her home was a long, long way away in a place called Haran, and her exciting story followed: 'One evening I had gone to draw water from the well, carrying my water-pitcher on my shoulder. I enjoyed going to the well because there I met my friends and I always picked up the latest bits of news and gossip. On this day I happened to be early and was the first there; I was surprised when a stranger came to me and asked for a drink of water. He was not a young man and I could see he had travelled a long way: his clothes were covered in dust and he looked tired. So I ran and filled my pitcher from the well and let him drink. He was so thirsty that he drank and drank. While he was drinking I saw that he had ten camels; I could see that they were especially fine animals and by their ornate trappings I knew that this man was someone special. The camels looked weary and I felt I had to give them some water too. So I told the man that I would draw water for his camels as well, if he wished, and I filled the water trough. You boys know how much thirsty camels drink' (two little heads nodded; they were so interested that they were afraid to speak and break the thread of the story). 'I filled my pitcher and poured it into the trough. You should have heard those camels grunting and honking as they gulped down the water faster than I could fill my pitcher. I don't know how many times I filled my pitcher before they stopped drinking. Then I had the surprise of my life: the stranger gave me the most beautiful nose ring I have ever seen and he put two solid gold bracelets on my wrists. Before I recovered from my amazement he asked me who my father was. When I told him I was the daughter of Bethuel, the son of Milcah, he bowed his head and worshipped the Lord.

'Then I discovered he was the servant of your grandfather, Abraham, who had left Haran such a long time ago. I ran home to tell my brother Laban, who went to the well and brought the man back with him. He was excited to meet Abraham's servant. But I think that most of his excitement came from looking at the expensive jewellery the man had given me.

'Well boys,' she said, 'the sun is going down, so that's all for tonight; time to go to sleep. But tomorrow night I will show you the gold nose ring and bracelets the man gave me, and I will tell you the rest of the story about how I went on a long, long journey with this man, and met your father for the first time.' She kissed them goodnight and soon they were both dreaming about mysterious strangers in far away places, and treasures of gold.

The next evening, the boys – for once – needed no persuading to go to bed; they were eager to hear the rest of the story, and to see the gold jewellery their mother had promised to show them. She had not forgotten and before entering called out, 'Are you ready?' They were, but when she entered dressed in a beautiful garment they had not seen before, and wearing her two magnificent gold bracelets, their eyes opened wide. She took off her bracelets and handed one to each of them so that they could feel their weight and examine the fine workmanship. Young as they were, they knew that they were worth a great deal, enough to buy many, many sheep.

'Now, where was I?' she asked, to be told immediately by the two of them in unison, 'You had just taken the stranger home to meet Uncle Laban.' She could not help smiling, so proud was she of her boys. Without further delay she continued her story.

'My brother Laban got the servants to prepare a meal but the stranger said he would not eat anything until he had told us the reason why he had come. He said that Abraham, your father's father, was now a wealthy man. Sarah (your grandfather Abraham's wife) had died and Abraham was now very old, and his son, Isaac, was forty years old but still not married. Abraham did not want Isaac to marry a Caananite woman, so he sent his servant to find our family and a bride for Isaac. The servant prayed and God guided him to the well near our home. He then prayed that the first woman who came to the well should be the one God had chosen. And, as a further sign, he prayed that when he asked for a drink she would also offer to draw water for his camels. Yes, you've guessed – I was that young woman, and soon I was on an exciting journey to Abraham's home. My brother Laban wanted to hold back my departure, but the servant insisted that we must not delay. So, when they agreed that it was up to me to decide, I told them I would go immediately.

'It was a long, long journey, but I was so excited that it didn't seem like it. When we arrived in the early evening I noticed a man walking and praying in the fields. I asked who he was (though in my heart I somehow knew the answer) and, sure enough, the servant said that he was Isaac, Abraham's son and heir. As soon as I saw him I knew I had made the right decision: he was handsome but, more important, he looked kind. He welcomed me and we have loved each other ever since.

'Well boys, that's the end of the story and time for you to go to sleep.'

One day, some three or four years later, the younger twin who had definitely become his mother's favourite, was helping her prepare a special meal for Isaac (who had become fond of his food). She sensed that he was not happy about something and so she asked him if he and his brother Esau had been quarrelling again. It had become almost a daily occurrence to find them arguing and, all too often, fighting as well. She didn't worry about that too much because she knew that it was the same with the children of many of her servants, who were always asking her for advice – it was part of growing up. When her two boys were fighting or wrestling, Esau nearly always won; but when it came to a battle of wits, he was no match for his younger twin, who would outsmart him nineteen times out of twenty, which always made Esau very angry.

She carried on preparing the food, knowing that whatever was troubling her younger son would soon come pouring out. And it did. He was upset because his older brother kept calling him a cheat, saying that his name, Jacob, actually meant cheat. He wanted his mother to tell him how he could change his name because he hated being called a cheat. She stopped what she was doing, hugged him and promised that as soon as she had finished preparing the meal she would sit down and tell him how he and his brother got their names.

She sat Jacob on her knee (Esau had long decided that he was too big to sit on her knee any more: he wanted to be a great hunter and hunters did not sit on Mother's knee) and told him he was old enough now to understand the mysterious story behind his name. After she had married Isaac they were both disappointed because after several years they still did not have any children. Isaac prayed and God answered the cry of his heart. Rebekah became pregnant and eventually felt a struggle in her womb. She prayed and asked God to explain what was happening. The answer he gave her was that she was carrying not one child but two, that they would form two nations, and 'one people will be stronger than the other, and the older will serve the younger'.

Rebekah told Jacob that when the day came for him and his brother to be born, the first baby came out red all over like a hairy garment; so they called him Esau, which means 'hairy'. Then she told how, when Jacob was born immediately afterwards, his hand took hold of Esau's heel; so he was given the name Jacob, meaning 'supplanter'. She agreed that it was not a pleasant name, but now he would understand the meaning behind it. Although he was the younger, his older brother would one day have to serve him. Young Jacob believed what his mother had told him and intended to do all in his power to make sure that it would come to pass.

The years seemed to fly by and all too soon for Rebekah her two sons were no longer boys, but men. Their father, Isaac, taught them how to keep sheep, how to dig wells, which trees to plant and where (he told them he had learned much of this from Abraham). He also got some of his servants – who were versed in military arts – to teach the young men how to use a bow, and also how to ride mules, donkeys and camels. Rebekah sensed that although her sons were growing up they were also growing further and further apart, as their interests differed:

Esau's first love was hunting, and his second was young women – especially the voluptuous Canaanite ones; Jacob enjoyed quieter pursuits such as home life, cooking, sheep rearing and well-digging. He had developed a special interest in the spiritual side of the birthright. He often asked Rebekah questions about it, but she usually referred him to his father. Isaac told Jacob more stories about Abraham, how God had called him to leave his fine home in Ur of the Chaldees, and to break away from the moon worshippers there, to trust the one true and living God. Jacob persuaded his father to tell him about the day he was spared at the last minute from being sacrificed by Abraham on the altar on Mount Moriah. And how God showed him a ram caught in the thicket by its horns, and directed him to offer this in Isaac's place. Afterwards Abraham told Isaac how God had given him a wonderful glimpse into the future about the Coming One, the Lamb of God, the Promised Deliverer, who would be a descendant of Isaac.

Isaac explained to both his sons what the birthright meant – that it was not something that one could see, or touch, like gold or earthly treasures. It centred mainly on their spiritual heritage – God's wonderful promises to Abraham, including also being the priest of the family, and the communicator of divine secrets. Most important of all it was a link in the line of descent by which the Promised Messiah would be born into the world. Jacob listened intently – for he sensed that the birthright was something very special indeed – and he wanted it, although he did not fully understand it. Esau, on the other hand, was bored by it all; his world ended at the horizon – the world one could see and feel and hold in one's hands; he was not concerned about praying to someone invisible; he got his excitement from chasing animals that could be caught and killed and eaten.

The passing years saw Isaac growing old, and eventually he became virtually blind. So he decided it was time to settle his affairs with his older son concerning the inheritance. He called Esau to him and asked him to go out hunting and return with venison to eat. (Isaac's taste for wild game was one of the reasons why he was so fond of Esau.) He told Esau that after his favourite meal he would bestow his blessing upon him. Esau did not waste a moment, for he never needed any urging to go hunting. Now at last he was going to get his rightful inheritance, his double portion. That would put his cheating brother Jacob in his place. But living in a tent meant that it was almost impossible to keep anything secret and Rebekah overheard everything. She was disappointed in Isaac: he knew that God had revealed before the twins were born that the elder would serve the younger. She would make sure it would happen.

Shortly after his fortieth birthday Esau had married two Canaanite women. For Rebekah this was the last straw: Esau's two wives were making Rebekah's and Isaac's lives miserable. Rebekah found Jacob and unfolded her clever plot. Isaac's ageing taste buds would never know the difference between her kid-stew and Esau's venison, so she despatched Jacob to kill two of their young goats. She cut off the choicest pieces and, while the stew was cooking, dressed Jacob in Esau's best clothes, covering his smooth hands and neck with the goatskins. Jacob, although afraid of his father discovering the trick they were playing on him, went ahead with Rebekah's scheme. And, despite some anxious moments, Isaac was duped into giving Esau's blessing to Jacob. No sooner had Jacob left his father's presence than Esau returned, cooked the venison and took it to his father. When Isaac realised what had happened he trembled, not so much with anger at Jacob, but because he remembered the prophecy given before the twins were born. Isaac knew that he had been guilty of ignoring God's word concerning Jacob, the younger twin. As for Esau, he wept bitter tears of disappointment, which quickly turned into murderous hatred of Jacob: as soon as the time was ripe he would kill his cheating brother.

Rebekah got wind of Esau's murderous threats and asked Isaac to send Jacob away to her brother Laban to find a wife there. Isaac readily agreed because he was deeply grieved at the horrible behaviour of his Canaanite daughters-in-law, and hoped Jacob would find a suitable wife for himself from his mother's family. Rebekah could hardly bear to part from her favourite son, but she comforted herself with the assurance that Esau's anger would die down and before long it would be safe for Jacob to return. She watched her dear home-loving son start the long, five-hundred-mile journey; she stood and strained her eyes to follow every heart-rending step taking him further and further away from her. She little knew that it was the final parting – he would return a very different person, but not in her lifetime.

It was the first time Jacob had left home, but he walked quickly; he took Esau's threats seriously and frequently looked back over his shoulder. He knew he could never outrun his brother and also realised it was no use trying to cover his tracks: he had seen Esau's skill in following an apparently invisible trail.

Jacob hurried on in spite of his exhaustion; but night came at last and he felt it was safe to lie down and rest. He lay down and the day's walking ensured that sleep came swiftly. Not even his troubled mind was a match for his weary body. While asleep he dreamed that he saw a ladder reaching all the way up to heaven, with angels of God ascending and descending on it. The Lord himself stood above it and said, 'I am the LORD, the God of your father Abraham and the God of Isaac. I will give you and your descendants the land on which you are lying' (Genesis 28:13). The next morning when Jacob woke up he knew that God was there with him, and he named the place Bethel, 'house of God'. He made a promise that if God would be with him, keep him, and bring him safely home again in peace, the Lord would be his God.

There was now a spring in his step and within a month he

reached his destination. Seeing some shepherds with their sheep around a well, the mouth covered by a large stone, he asked them where they had come from. Learning that they lived in Haran, he asked if they knew Laban. Yes, they did and it just so happened that the young woman approaching with her sheep was Laban's daughter, Rachel. Ever the opportunist, Jacob rolled the great stone off the well and proceeded to draw water for Rachel's flock. The astonished Rachel next found herself being kissed by this gallant stranger, who with tears in his eyes told her he was the son of Laban's sister, Rebekah. She immediately took to her heels and ran home shouting excitedly, 'Father! Father! Cousin Jacob, Aunt Rebekah's son, is here.' Laban hastened to the well and welcomed his nephew with hugs and kisses – it was Jacob's turn to be astonished – and pleased.

The first glimpse of young Rachel had set his heart beating faster than he could ever remember. She was so beautiful and so like his mother. He had heard the stories about the stunning beauty of Isaac's mother, Sarah, who, even though in her eighties, had been wooed by Pharaoh, King of Egypt. But Jacob was sure that Rachel was the most beautiful of all. For the first time in his life he knew he was falling in love. Laban insisted that he stay with them and over the next month Jacob knew with every passing day, and every sight and sound of Rachel, that he wanted to marry her. The attraction was mutual; this clever cousin who had arrived so unexpectedly had made an immediate impression by his show of skill and strength in rolling the great stone off the well, by his drawing water for her flock. She was in love and began to dream of marriage.

At the end of that first month Jacob asked Laban for his daughter's hand. The wily old Laban, who had been watching Jacob, soon realised that Jacob was a skilled worker and besotted with Rachel. Laban put his arm around his nephew's shoulder and, with a plausibility that came naturally after years of practice, said that just because Jacob was a blood-relative did not mean that Laban could ever take advantage of him by not paying him a wage. 'Tell me,' he said, and with such an innocent smile that he almost believed it himself, 'what wages would you like?' Jacob could not believe his good fortune and responded, 'I will serve you seven years for Rachel.' 'Done,' said Laban, turning away to hide his smug smile; he knew he had just negotiated the best seven-year wage agreement he had ever made with a worker.

Jacob still thought he had got the best of the bargain and was so much in love that the seven years passed like only a few days. Then the time came for his beloved Rachel to become his wife. The unsuspecting Jacob could think of nothing else but his first night alone with Rachel. What a feast Laban put on! The feasting seemed to go on and on, but night fell and at last he was alone with his beloved.

However, the night before has a nasty habit of being followed by a bright and all too early morning after. Jacob could not understand why his beloved wife kept hiding under the bedclothes; he so wanted to take her lovely face in his hands and assure her of his love over and over again. At last his wife emerged from beneath the bedclothes and his expressions of love and devotion died on his lips, for it was Rachel's older sister Leah! Jacob's anger blazed within him: Laban had tricked him.

Dressing hurriedly he ran to find his cunning uncle, who greeted him with such sympathy and understanding that Jacob was almost taken in again. Laban had the amazing ability to make anything sound plausible: he apologised, but in his country it was unthinkable for the younger daughter to be married before the elder, and Leah would make him such a good wife. If he wanted he could still have Rachel – after another seven years' service! Once Leah's wedding week of feasting was ended Jacob could marry Rachel.

Jacob caught a glimpse of a red-eyed Rachel in the background and he knew that she was all he wanted. What was another seven years compared to such a love as his for Rachel? In a moment she was in his arms, sobbing as though her heart would break as she explained that her father had forced her to do it; she was afraid that Jacob would hate her; she had wept all night thinking of Leah with Jacob. Laban waited, then, with a gentle hand on Jacob's shoulder, simply said, 'Agreed then? Seven more years?' 'Agreed,' said Jacob, waving him away. Laban went away, rubbing his hands over another smart wage settlement – what a pity he hadn't got another daughter.

Poor Rachel had spent a night of agony and frustration, forced to go along with his devious plot; Leah, of course, had needed no persuading – it was her right as the elder daughter to be married first. She was sure she could make Jacob love her, but she soon realised her mistake; Jacob did not come near her again during that week; his one thought was for Rachel.

Once Jacob had managed to pacify Rachel, his anger against Laban reasserted itself. The miserable old cheat! Suddenly Jacob realised how Esau had felt; he understood for the first time why his brother had wanted to kill him. Every time he looked at Uncle Laban it was like looking at a mirror image of himself; and Jacob did not like what he saw.

Jacob and Rachel were so in love that Jacob's second seven-year term of service to Laban seemed to pass fairly quickly. There was only one shadow over their happiness: Rachel failed to become pregnant. She was jealous when her sister Leah presented Jacob with his first son, whom she named Reuben – confident that now her husband would love her. She soon discovered otherwise, though, and not even a second son, Simeon, or a third son, Levi, or a fourth son, Judah, changed things between Leah and Jacob. The effect upon Rachel, however, was devastating; she became desperate and gave her handmaid, Bilhah, to Jacob, to bear a child on her behalf. Bilhah duly presented them with another son, Dan. If Rachel thought this would improve matters she was sadly mistaken; Leah in turn presented her handmaid, Zilpah, to Jacob, resulting in another son, Gad; followed in due course with yet another son, Asher.

Leah was sure that happiness would be hers at last, but not so. Even when she herself produced two more sons, Issachar and Zebulun, and a daughter, Dinah, things remained the same: Jacob remained committed to her, but it was Rachel he really loved. And when his beloved Rachel finally produced a child herself, named Joseph, Leah knew things between her and Jacob would never be any different.

When Jacob finally completed his fourteen years of service he told Laban he felt it was time for him to leave and go back home, but Laban was reluctant to let him go because Jacob had made him richer than he had ever been. The scheming Laban made a new agreement and during the next six years tried every trick he could think of, including decreasing Jacob's wages ten times! In spite of it all, Jacob prospered, not because of his own efforts to outsmart Uncle Laban, but because the God of Abraham was watching over him and teaching him that there was a better way than cheating – the way of faith, obedience and trust in the living God.

One day God spoke to Jacob and he knew that it was time to leave Laban. But he faced a greater fear: meeting up with his twin brother Esau again. He sent on ahead some of his best men and instructed them to greet Esau with smooth words a seasoned diplomat would have found it impossible to better. It was all to no avail, however, as the return message made Jacob panic: Esau was coming to meet him with four hundred men!

Jacob divided his large following into two main groups, preceded by several groups of servants with extravagant gifts of goats, sheep, camels and cattle for Esau – hoping to buy or bribe his way out of trouble. He feared that Esau would kill not only him, but also his wives, children and his whole company. His wives and children would bring up the rear, Leah first – a position for once she did not want; whereas Rachel and Joseph, his favoured wife and favourite son, would be at the back in the safest possible place – as far away from danger as possible, and with the best means of escape.

That night, having checked his plans yet again, Jacob went out into the darkness; he needed to be alone to think and to pray. Suddenly he was aware of another presence. Who was it? Was it a spy from Esau? No, this was no ordinary visitor – he experienced the same overwhelming Presence as on his first night away from home when he had seen the angels and the ladder to heaven. This, however, was no dream, and the one who faced him now, though in human form, was obviously more than a mere man. All night the heavenly visitor stayed and wrestled with Jacob, who discovered more about himself, and about God, than in the whole of his life. As he wrestled, in some mysterious way Jacob's thigh was touched and put out of joint. As the first gleam of dawn appeared on the eastern horizon, the heavenly visitor made to leave, but Jacob clung to him desperately, knowing that this was the only one who could really help him. When Jacob refused to let him go until he had blessed him, the visitor – so awesome, so mighty, so knowing, yet so gentle – asked his name. Ashamed to own it, he told him, 'It is Jacob.' And even as he spoke it he could hear Esau's voice echoing in his soul, shouting, 'Cheat! Cheat! Cheat!' He could hardly believe his ears when the visitor said, 'Your name will no longer be Jacob, but Israel, because you have struggled with God and with men and have overcome' (Genesis 32:28). Jacob called the place Peniel, for he said, 'It is because I saw God face to face, and yet my life was spared' (Genesis 32:30).

Jacob limped his wondering way back to his waiting family and even as he arrived he could see Esau and his band of four hundred men bearing down upon them. Jacob went ahead of his wives and children to meet Esau – and bowed before his brother trembling. What would Esau do now? To the astonishment of all present Esau dismounted, ran to his twin brother and hugged and kissed him; the two of them stood there embracing each other with tears streaming down their faces.

Jacob's love for Rachel never wavered and when she became pregnant again his joy overflowed. But it was a difficult birth and, though the baby boy was delivered safely, there was nothing the midwife could do to save Rachel. With her last breath she named her newborn son Benoni, 'son of my sorrow'; but the bereaved Jacob changed it to Benjamin, 'son of my right hand'. His beloved Rachel at the cost of her life had given him a most precious gift. Jacob sorrowed as he laid her body to rest, and marked the grave with a pillar. It was a place he would never forget – so near to Bethlehem. Was it only his imagination as he wept over the loss of the love of his life, his precious Rachel, that one day in the far distant future the full significance of Bethlehem would unfold?

In Egypt many years later Jacob, who knew that he would not live much longer, gathered his twelve sons around him to give them his final blessings and a revelation from God of what the future had in store for them. Jacob, along with all God's prophets, was looking forward to the coming of the Promised One, the Saviour of the world. Abraham, Isaac and Jacob spent their lives looking forward in faith to the coming of the Messiah and, in the fullness of time, he came to Bethlehem.

# 7

## Colin and Hazel Whittaker

London was an exciting place to be in November 1947; it was the focus of attention, not only for the nation, but for the world. Most people love a wedding and the forthcoming marriage of HRH Princess Elizabeth and the Duke of Edinburgh captured the popular imagination. Although the war had finished in 1945, austerity and rationing remained. But here at last was a glorious excuse for everyone to break free and celebrate a royal wedding in style.

London was ablaze with colour and crowded with sight-seers – including my parents who had come down from Rochdale, Lancashire, for the occasion. I was doubly excited because in a few short weeks I was due to be demobbed from the Royal Army Medical Corps after serving three and a half years, following my call-up, aged eighteen years, in June 1944. I had spent the previous year and a half at a branch of the War Office, serving as a corporal under Lt Col J. Irvine Fortescue, DSO, dealing with the resettlement of Polish army doctors. It was a wonderful time for me; the colonel had a distinguished service record and, though a strict disciplinarian, was fair. Although I had learned much from serving under him I was convinced that my posting to London from Northern Ireland was a wonderful answer to prayer.

Fred Town from Rochdale, a valet to Lord Dudley in London's Belgravia, had been brought to know Christ as his Saviour through an open-air meeting conducted by Peniel Chapel at the famous Speakers' Corner, Hyde Park. On a visit home to Rochdale he went to the pioneer Assembly of God church, where my parents attended. His glowing reports of Peniel Chapel reached me in Ireland by means of my parents' letters and I had a witness in my heart that this was where God wanted me to be. I approached my commanding officer about the chance of a posting to London and was told in no uncertain terms that I would never get one. However, within a matter of two or three weeks a posting came through for 'One Clerk Orderly Clinical to be sent to London forthwith' – I was the only one of that grading at the large military hospital at Moira, County Down!

As soon as I arrived in London on my first free weekend I attended Peniel Chapel and found it all and more than Fred had described. The godly old pastor, Ben Griffiths, had been blessed by God's Spirit in a remarkable way in the Welsh Revival of 1904 and in due course had been led to London. He owned a dairy, but immediately pioneered a new ministry that soon grew to become Peniel Chapel. He was around seventy-eight years of age when I met him, but still very much in charge of the well-attended church. Peniel, in spite of the war, still maintained a strong, active congregation of around three hundred, with missionaries in Brazil, China, and elsewhere. The church also had an amazing tract-distribution ministry, open-air meetings every night of the week, except Friday, plus numerous prayer meetings, Bible studies and testimony meetings.

Being at a branch of the War Office I had the most comfortable hours of all my army service: 9.30 a.m. to 5 p.m. I revelled in them and found myself free in the evening to preach with Peniel members almost every night of the week in Hyde Park, seeking always to point souls to Christ and, if possible, to get them to return with us afterwards to the chapel. Of my many contacts I especially remember two: an official from the Iraqi Embassy (a Muslim), and a fairly high-up trade union official. I was at all the prayer meetings and Pastor Griffiths gave me much encouragement, affording me opportunities to preach. When the time approached for me to be demobbed he solemnly charged me in his wonderful Welsh voice, 'Make full proof of your ministry.' He then startled me by telling me that he had some money to come from war damage and that if I was willing to stay on at Peniel after my discharge from the Royal Army Medical Corps, after a year he would send me out evangelising.

I was encouraged and humbled by his offer, but after prayer felt that I first had to return home to Rochdale. I considered writing to Pastor George Oldershaw, Chairman of Assembly of God Home Missions, under whom I had served for three and a half months as a trainee evangelist before my call-up. With the brashness of youth I was going to write to him to ask him to send me to the hardest place so that I could prove my calling! Mercifully for me that letter was never written. Instead, I arrived home in Rochdale to find the struggling new assembly without a pastor and somehow I found myself spending the eight weeks of my demob leave acting as (unpaid!) pastor. I immediately put into practice much of what I had learned at Peniel and God graciously blessed us. We saw some increase as we instituted half-nights of prayer, regular door-to-door visitation and distribution of gospel tracts, open-air meetings on the Town Hall square, Bible studies, midweek children's meetings, as well as the Sunday school that my mother had started, which was doing well.

When my demob leave ended (and with it my army pay) I felt that I should not leave until a new pastor had been appointed. So, as a temporary measure, I went out and got a job as a clerk to support myself until that happened, after which I could decide where my future lay. There was again an opportunity for me to attend a teacher training college and go into teaching, but I knew that God had called me to the ministry and dared not disobey. After working for only a few weeks, the growing nucleus of faithful members met together and then approached me with an offer to support me if I would take on the pastorate full-time. The support was small, but I was single and living with my parents. It was sufficient and I sought to justify their confidence in me by working far harder than I had ever done in the army. I rose early to pray, studied hard, fasted regularly, and God graciously helped us with some great workers. One young man, Ken Reid, joined me and we met every Friday for half-nights of prayer, inviting any who felt the burden for revival and lost souls to join us.

Those early days were not without incident. We arranged for a week's campaign with the evangelist from Peniel Chapel, Harold Miles, another who had found Christ through Peniel's open-air meetings in Hyde Park. The hired hall in which the pioneer assembly met was in the centre of the town, on the first floor, over a café. On the Saturday afternoon the campaign started we had arranged to meet for prayer before going out to distribute invitation leaflets to the shoppers. As we prayed there was a terrific thunderstorm with loud claps of thunder and very heavy rain. (Much as I would like to think it was the result of our earnest, Pentecostal-style praying, I am sure that was not the case!)

After praying, as we waited for the rain to abate, I went into a room we used as a vestry across the other side of the stairs. To my astonishment the door was in splinters and wide open. My first thought was that lightning had struck it, but I soon found we had been burgled, and the noise of the break-in had been masked by the thunder. We had left our overcoats in that room, all apart from evangelist Harold Miles who had hung his new raincoat inside the main hall. As it was still raining heavily, he volunteered to fetch the police.

While waiting for him to return I went into the café below to ask the lady at the till if she had seen any sign of the thief. She hadn't, but before our evangelist returned with a policeman, she called me back to inform me that a man who had left the café a short while before not wearing a raincoat, had now returned wearing one and was sitting in the café with his friends. I looked and recognised the raincoat he was wearing as my demob raincoat. I went in with the policeman who challenged the man and suggested we should talk outside. Being a polite Rochdale policeman he signalled that the man should go first, whereupon the accused was out of the door in a flash, pursued by the policeman, me and Harold Miles (the latter, being somewhat rotund in shape, abandoned his chase at the first corner, all of five yards away!).

Being young and still fit from the army, I soon overtook the policeman. The thief, who was running very fast (I learned in due course that he had played professional rugby league for St Helens), went up into the crowded main street leading to the market. The policeman was shouting, 'Stop that thief!' and as I was by then some five or six yards ahead of the policeman and the thief was some ten yards ahead of me, one brave citizen assumed that I was the wanted man and duly tripped me and sent me sprawling in the wet.

I picked myself up, now looking very dishevelled, but still ahead of the policeman, who continued shouting, 'Stop that thief!' All who recognised me in the market wondered what I had been up to. The thief turned into a corner of the market hoping to find an exit, but instead found himself trapped; so he was caught and handcuffed. The *Rochdale Observer* headed one of its inside columns 'Whilst at prayer . . . thief robs church . . .'

But that was not quite the end of the story. When the case came up at the Magistrate's Court we learned that the thief had pawned the stolen things and then returned to pay the bill in the café where his two pals were waiting. The list of stolen items was duly read out – one raincoat, one small suitcase containing a pair of pink bedroom slippers, one alarm clock, and so on, much to everyone's amusement.

The latter items belonged to Hazel Lee, who with her friend Joan Fitton had become a regular at the church. Hazel spent most weekends at Joan's home so that they could attend the 7 a.m. prayer meeting we held on Sunday mornings. Hazel and Joan had been converted the previous year at a Cliff College crusade and had proved the reality of their new-found faith. That was the first time Hazel had heard the gospel truly preached. Cliff College staff evangelist Tom Butler ministered, his preaching of the cross of Christ reducing her to tears. Hazel responded as soon as he made the appeal. Before then she had spent every spare evening in the local ballroom; she was an excellent dancer and loved dancing, but though no one spoke a word to her, after her conversion she never returned to the ballroom.

Hazel deeply impressed me with her devotion and commitment to Christ and her faithfulness in prayer and readiness to speak about him. She was a nursery nurse and had succeeded in bringing all her colleagues to hear the gospel. Although she had to face a lot of opposition at home, she never wavered. Her father, a sergeant major during the war, had just returned home after years overseas, and on the night of her conversion when she went home and witnessed to her family he responded sceptically, 'I will give you two weeks.'

In due course I was accepted as a probationer by the Lancashire District Council of the Assemblies of God, and I continued to study and work as hard as possible to prove my calling. After several months of careful observation and prayer I was fully convinced that Hazel was the young lady I wanted to marry. Although I had never dated her, so sure was I that she was the one for me, I asked if I might talk with her. I then told her I wanted to marry her. In her ballroom dancing days Hazel was regularly asked for dates, but this was a new approach for her! Fortunately for me she realised my proposal, although sudden, was serious, and to my joy and relief she said 'yes'. I was clear in my own mind and heart that this would have to wait until I had finished my period as a probationer minister. In the interim our courtship would, of necessity, be severely restricted, as the ministry had to take priority over everything else.

As events transpired our courtship turned out to be even more testing for both of us than I could have imagined. I soon found myself under subtle pressures from my parents and key groups in the small church. In the few weeks in which Hazel and I had time to strengthen our relationship before the pressure really mounted, I knew I was in love and Hazel responded as wholeheartedly and seriously as I had hoped. The suggestions from those around me were made in ways I found hard to ignore – especially those who hinted that it was too soon to get married when I was still seeking to prove my ministry. Ultimately, I felt I had to surrender the love of my life, for that is what Hazel had already become to me. The more I learned about her character and commitment, the more certain I was that she was God's gift to me. It was with a sad heart that I tried to explain to Hazel that I felt that we should break off our relationship for the time being.

The following twenty months were some of the most testing of my life, as I believe they were for Hazel also. She continued faithfully to attend all the services and so we were constantly in contact with each other, but having to keep ourselves totally separate. More than once my heart sank as I feared that I would lose her to another. Several of my young ministerial colleagues who, like me, were just starting out in the ministry, sought an explanation as to why I had 'given up' such a treasure of a person. One or two expressed it in very non-theological terms: I was 'nuts'! If Hazel had given an opening, I know they would have been only too ready to make their approaches to court her. I held my breath, miserable and afraid, my faith as well as my love severely tested, knowing more certainly than ever that Hazel was the one I wanted to share my life with.

Fortunately for me, Hazel still loved me and, although she was approached by at least one hopeful, she remained steadfastly unattached. But for how long? I believed that soon we would be together again and we talked about it briefly. Hazel understandably asked, 'How long before that happens?' I could only answer that I did not know, but felt that God had spoken to me from Psalm 37:4, which I shared with her: 'Delight yourself in the LORD and he will give you the desires of your heart.' I tried to assure her that I still had to wait for God somehow to set his seal upon this.

Within days two letters arrived, one from Ben Griffiths at Peniel with the words 'I think that the young lady with the face like an angel would make you an excellent wife' (Hazel had visited Peniel many months previously). The other was from Leeds, from my older brother Robert, who was at the teacher training college following his demob. He said that he thought Hazel would make me a good wife. It was the confirmation I had waited for. At the first opportunity I was proposing again to my beloved Hazel, but this time with an engagement ring and serious discussion about a wedding day. To my relief and joy, she accepted and the date was fixed for 2nd September 1950.

Evangelist Harold Miles officiated and one of our hymns was Charles Wesley's 'Love Divine, all loves excelling'. It was a wonderful service where we pledged our love to one another and our united lives to serving Christ.

We spent the first few days of our honeymoon at the home of two more friends from Peniel Chapel, Mr and Mrs William Tubby. A regular soldier and a warrant officer, it was while he was on the staff of an Officer Training Unit in the north of England that he, along with his wife, had been wonderfully converted. He and his wife were two of the most dedicated personal workers I have ever met. After the war he was accepted as a Beefeater at the Tower of London. Even when conducting tours round the Tower he would always manage to slip in a witness to Christ as Saviour and Lord, in such a way that it was impossible to take offence, yet making a telling point.

To begin our honeymoon we travelled down to London by train and got a taxi to take us to the Tower. It was then 10 p.m., and dark, and the taxi driver gave us some strange looks as we stood with our suitcases outside the locked gates; he seemed rather glad to get away. The gate was guarded by a formidable-looking Guardsman, wearing a great black busby and armed with a bayoneted rifle. I told him that we were expected – but he stood there, rigid and silent. Fortunately for us Mr Tubby arrived, just as we were wondering whether we were going to have to spend the first night of our honeymoon on the pavement at Tower Hill. He gave the guard the password (which is issued daily by the Governor of the Tower, but only to authorised staff) and the locked gates opened. Soon we were in their quarters and receiving the warmest and most loving of Christian welcomes – and we knew that not only our honeymoon but our married life was off to a memorable start.

Sunday found me preaching at Peniel and Hazel singing a solo, as well as speaking at one of the open-air services. It was a busy but beautiful day and the start of a pattern of life in the ministry that was to continue in similar vein.

From the Tower we went not to the block but to Littlehampton in Sussex to the new home of my brother and his wife and child, where he had just commenced his teaching career. Our honeymoon ended as unusually as it had begun. I had promised that we would have a meal on the train from London to Manchester, and we enjoyed a marvellous dinner, spoiled only by the bill. I had budgeted for this, but during our honeymoon week the price had gone up. Fortunately I had enough to pay the bill, but was becoming a little anxious as funds dipped. We travelled by bus from Manchester to Rochdale only to find that during our honeymoon the fare on Manchester buses had also risen! Providentially for us the conductor told us that the fare rise applied only to the Manchester boundary and the fare after the Rochdale boundary was unchanged. I counted out my remaining money and after paying our fares was left with exactly one halfpenny (in old money that is). That halfpenny was all we had left to start our post-honeymoon life together, but we arrived in the house to find a letter from the Inland Revenue and a refund on my tax (now that I was a married man) for £5. If she did not know it before, Hazel was quickly discovering that life as the wife of a Pentecostal pastor was full of the unexpected, and never dull.

We started our married life sharing the home of my parents, as my older brother and his new wife had also done. Life for those returning home after the war was not easy and we were all most grateful to them. However, in the spring of 1951 I received an invitation to become the pastor of the Radcliffe Full Gospel Tabernacle, another Assembly of God church. It was a purpose-built church with a membership of around sixty. When the building was erected a few years before the war, the treasurer and his wife had willingly mortgaged their own home to make it possible. Their solicitor told them they were crazy, but God did not fail them – churches built with that kind of sacrifice and faith are certain to be blessed.

We were soon conscious that God was with us in this move. We were also favoured in that the church had a small manse, which was a real bonus for us. The expectations demanded of a pastor and his wife in that immediate post-war period were considerable, although the salary was not! This provided us with endless opportunities to exercise our faith, but neither Hazel nor I would have missed those early days of testing. The concept of one-man-ministry prevailed, which meant that the pastor did all the preaching, and what he did not do his wife was expected to do. But we were young, enthusiastic and full of faith, so this did not bother us.

The week consisted of preaching Sunday morning and evening, with Sunday school in the afternoon, Monday evening was the prayer meeting, Wednesday the Bible study, Friday was the youth night, Saturday the testimony meeting. There was also a midweek meeting for children on Wednesday evenings before the Bible study, which was to be taken by the pastor's wife. Preparing at least three new sermons every week ensured that I put in lots of hours in my study. I was also informed that one more duty the pastor had to perform was to attend to the coke-fired church boiler. That was a new experience for me, but I soon learned to deal with the boiler, especially if by some mischance it had gone out and the congregation arrived to a cold church! And, in case we had any spare time on our hands, we were expected to visit the congregation members on a regular basis. Nevertheless, we loved it. The church grew slowly but steadily and it was a memorable day when the congregation first reached the hundred mark.

Then we organised an evangelistic crusade by the much-blessed Welsh evangelist Howell Harris (named after the great eighteenth-century evangelist). The campaign was so successful that we had to extend the two weeks into four. The follow-up of the new converts and the verification of those who said that they had been healed pushed us to the limits. The reward was to find some thirty or forty new converts who proved genuine, along with some definite cases of healing. Here again there were remarkable incidents. One I shall never forget is a lady of about sixty who started attending, but only occasionally. One day she felt she owed me an explanation and said, 'I will start attending regularly when my husband is dead!' She went on to explain that he was opposed to her attending our services. However, over the months his attitude softened and when she did attend he started meeting her outside the church. We prayed and eventually he came with her and surrendered his life to Christ. The change in his life was both instantaneous and dramatic. He was older than her and within a short time was found to have terminal cancer of the throat (he had been a lifelong, heavy smoker). His wife was at his bedside just before his death and described how he suddenly opened his eyes and with great feeling and all his dying strength declared, 'No, Satan, you cannot have me. I did belong to you, but now I belong to Jesus.' Shortly afterwards he slipped peacefully away.

In the summer of 1952, to our joy, Hazel became pregnant, but it was soon clear that she was not well. It was only when we had a Peniel missionary as a guest speaker that the root of the trouble was spotted. The missionary, Henry Leith, had been sent out to China by Peniel Chapel. When Japan entered the war he, his wife and baby daughter were placed in a camp for enemy aliens. The conditions were terrible: they had to boil grass and strain off the juices to try to feed their baby daughter. Many died around them, starved to death for the most part; but through prayer, courage and God's help, the Leiths survived. He had seen so many people suffering with anaemia that within a few hours of being in our home he told me, 'You must do something urgently – Hazel is on the brink of pernicious anaemia.' A visit to our doctor confirmed the serious situation and Hazel was given iron injections and a diet was prescribed.

The baby was not expected until April 1953, but early on Sunday morning, 22nd February 1953, Hazel woke me with the news that her waters had broken. The ambulance took her to the local maternity home from which I was excluded – fathers were not allowed anywhere near the labour ward in those days. The expected birth was regarded as insufficient reason for me not to preach at the communion service! As soon as possible after the service I phoned the maternity home. The matron had given instructions that when I phoned she was the one who had to answer. I asked if she had any news for me and she replied, 'Yes, you are the proud father of a little girl, *and a little boy!*'

I dashed across the town to the maternity home to get the full story. Hazel told me exactly what had happened. At 10.15 a.m. the doctor had delivered a baby girl and then said, 'I think there's another baby here.' Five minutes later he delivered a baby boy. They were six and a half weeks premature and that was the first inkling that Hazel was carrying twins. When I first saw them they were wrapped in cotton wool in an oxygen tent. They were beautiful, but tiny, and as I stood admiring them, still trying to take it all in, the matron warned me, 'Now Reverend Whittaker, they are very tiny but, I promise you, if I keep them a week, I will keep them.' She was true to her word and had our precious twins moved into her quarters so that she could watch over them personally. She insisted on Hazel breastfeeding them every three hours, round the clock. As they were so small it took them a long time to feed and Hazel, though so thrilled to have them in her arms, soon found herself totally exhausted.

When our doctor heard of the double birth he apologised and explained that, although he had wondered whether there might be twins, his examinations revealed only one heartbeat, one head, and so on. He also told me that the same thing had happened to his wife, and the leading specialist attending her had to be called back from the operating theatre to deliver the other twin baby.

Hazel was allowed home after three weeks, but Matron insisted that the twins could not come home until they had reached five pounds in weight. Hazel had to use a breast pump to draw off her milk and I had to deliver her to the maternity home twice daily! It was a trying time, especially for Hazel who longed to have her babies home. All we had in preparation for the birth was names. Early in the pregnancy we agreed that if the baby was a girl she would be named

Beryl Hazel, if a boy, Colin Wesley; but happy with either sex during the pregnancy we always referred to 'it' as Wesber.

Wesley was smaller at birth and for a time slipped below the three-pound mark. It seemed that the twins would never get to five pounds, but Matron finally agreed to allow them home, even though both were still some ounces too light. The condition was that Hazel had to agree to breastfeed them every three hours, around the clock. They took a long time to feed, and it seemed as if Hazel were on an endless treadmill. Many nights after feeding them she had night-mares, waking up terrified that she had fallen asleep while feeding one of them and had lain on them. At the end of six months she was exhausted and our doctor agreed to Hazel feeding them from a bottle. This made life easier and enabled me to assist in their feeding. In spite of everything God won-derfully undertook and Beryl and Wesley grew up very healthy, and have remained so to this day. The church also continued to grow.

1953 was Coronation Year, and having been made Youth Secretary for the Lancashire District, I had the exciting expe-rience of organising (with the help of two outstanding senior ministers, J. Nelson Parr and Eddie Durham) a great celebra-tion youth rally in the newly rebuilt Manchester Free Trade Hall. It was so successful that we had to hire the Methodist Albert Hall situated a few yards down on the opposite side of the street. This was so that we could run the two halves of the rally simultaneously by alternating the programmes and speakers for the afternoon and evening meetings. The atten-dance totalled over four thousand. I was still the pastor of the Radcliffe church; Youth Secretary was just another extra.

Teddy Hodgson, a great missionary with the Congo Evangelistic Mission (CEM) was home from the Belgian Congo and he dedicated our twins, Beryl and Wesley, to God. Sadly, in 1961 Teddy was martyred along with fellow mis-sionary Elton Knauf.

privileged to entertain in our home two more
gr          s linked with the CEM, James and Alice
Sa          pioneered the CEM in 1915 with another
fa          d, W.F.P. Burton, and Alice was the daugh-
te          an Smith Wigglesworth. Alice Salter was
st          famous father said it was because she
ha          n – but I'm sure that Smith Wigglesworth
w           s matter. Alice was a fantastic speaker and
could stir any congregation, especially when it came to missions. I had had the great privilege of corresponding with her
over a number of years and she was a wonderful encourager.

On the Sunday evening Mrs Salter said that she would
babysit and insisted that Hazel go to the service. Hazel was in
a quandary. We had chuckled as Mrs Salter had helped to dry
the dishes and cutlery after one meal, as she dropped more of
the dried cutlery onto the floor than into the drawer (she
could not hear it drop!). Hazel asked her, 'How will you hear
the twins if they cry?' She replied, 'Don't worry, I will go up
every few minutes and make sure they are all right – you go,
my dear, and don't worry.'

The impact of these wonderful Christians on our lives has
lasted. Mr Salter in his pioneering days with Mr Burton three
times had a sheet put over him as a corpse, but each time God
raised him up! Mr and Mrs Salter travelled the world with
Smith Wigglesworth and we were enthralled with the stories
they shared with us. Such fellowship is something money can
never buy.

During their stay with us at the time of the convention Mrs
Salter told the congregation, 'When Colin was a little boy I
slept in his bed and I claimed him for Congo – but you got him
instead.' It was the first I knew of that but was humbled and
blessed to know that such a person had prayed for me. Life in
God's service is truly wonderful.

A visit of Donald Gee at another Anniversary Convention
in Radcliffe resulted in his recommending us to his former

church in Edinburgh and, in 1957, we bade a tearful farewell to our precious Radcliffe congregation. Our stay in Edinburgh was mostly happy and memorable in many ways – but it was not easy. One day Hazel said to me, 'Beryl and Wesley will be grown up and in their twenties and we will only be in our early forties; and I've been thinking how nice it would be to have another baby. The twins are wonderful but it has been such hard work, and to have one would be easy.'

In due time Hazel became pregnant and we rejoiced in happy anticipation. Then one day as Hazel was at the doctor's for her monthly check-up, he chuckled but refused to say why. Next month he chuckled again and called in the nurse who examined Hazel and then chuckled too. 'Well?' demanded Hazel. The doctor and nurse were reticent, but Hazel realised that twins were possible again. It had never entered our heads that it could happen twice. Hazel insisted that she had to know, so we were sent up to the Edinburgh City Hospital for a scan. The news was that Hazel was bearing twins again! When she told one of the stalwart spinsters in the church, the good Scottish lady responded, 'Och no, Mrs Whittaker, that's impossible. You canna' have twins twice.' Once we got over the shock we were thrilled; at least this time we were prepared, and on 8th September 1959 Lois and Mark joined our happy family. They were four to five weeks premature but heavier at birth than our first twins, which made life a little easier. Hazel has been a wonderful mother; under her loving, wise and sacrificial care both sets of twins have prospered in every way. The fact that all four of our children have survived and done so well in life is due mainly to Hazel.

While in Edinburgh I became the editor of the Assemblies of God National Youth Magazine, *Pentecostal Youth*. Again it was an extra, unpaid job, but one I enjoyed and God graciously blessed.

After nearly six years in Edinburgh we accepted a call to pastor the Assemblies of God church in Bishop Auckland,

County Durham. Our four and a half years there seemed like a rest cure after our intense years in Edinburgh. Then a call to pastor the Assemblies of God church in Luton was accepted, with a united conviction that it was the right time and the right place, and so it proved for the next twelve years. They were wonderful years for us as a family, for the church, and for our ministry. Wynne Lewis (Elim General Superintendent) and Colin Urquhart were also led by the Lord to Luton some two years later, and we became firm friends, praying together regularly, and also playing cricket together on many occasions, as we all loved cricket. I was also privileged to be invited by Michael Harper to become part of the newly formed Charismatic Leaders' Conference. It was Michael who arranged for David DuPlessis to come to Luton for what turned out to be a truly memorable meeting. Those were the early days of the work of God's Spirit in the historic churches.

As the children were growing up Hazel could pursue her studies, and the way opened up for her to teach in private schools. While at Moorlands School, with the help and backing of the headmaster, Dr Whitlock, she was able to study and obtain her teaching qualifications. The title of Associate was conferred on her by the historic College of Preceptors. How Hazel managed to fit in the long hours of study while caring for the family, and still maintaining her church activities, I will never know. She could not have done this had she not had a hysterectomy soon after our arrival in Luton. Although the operation was successful and her general health rapidly improved, intense and frequent migraines began. Hazel has never been set free from these afflictions, but we believe that much prayer and her courage have enabled her to continue to live an amazingly full and busy life. And through it all, our love and appreciation for each other and our children and five grandchildren has continued to grow.

Our twelve happy years in Luton ended when I was elected to the full-time position of Editor of the Assemblies of God national magazine – then a weekly named *Redemption Tidings* – which necessitated our move to Nottingham. I retired in 1994, and Hazel and I daily thank God for his great goodness in bringing us together, and for the happy day in 1950 when we agreed to 'love and cherish each other, for better for worse, for richer for poorer, in sickness and in health, till death us do part'. Married life, 'according to God's holy ordinance', is the most wonderful and most satisfying way for a man and a woman to live together in this present world.

# Study Guide

# 1. Martin and Katrina Luther

## How should we prepare for marriage?

1. Did courtship/engagement help Katrina to realise she was in danger of marrying the wrong man (p. 16)? Do you admire Katrina's courage for ending the engagement, especially when potential suitors were not slow to remind her that she was already regarded as too old for marriage (p. 18)?

2. Martin was almost forty-two years old and Katrina twenty-six when they were married (p. 2). Does age difference matter, or is 'being of the same mind' more important? Can one be too young or too old for marriage?

3. Is marriage 'just a scrap of paper' or is it much more than a legal certificate? What does it mean for Christians? Are married people more likely to stay together? (Matthew 19: 5–6)

4. Martin was convinced that there was no reason why parish priests should practise celibacy if they preferred a married life. He also believed that nuns who had been forced to take vows in early years, without a definite sense of calling, were at liberty to leave their cloisters (p. 18). When is it better to marry than remain single (1 Corinthians 7)?

5. Although Luther had said that there had been no emotional or sexual fascination, once married he was soon enjoying Katrina's presence in both bed and house (p. 21). Luther had no inhibitions about the marriage bed and accepted it as pure and beautiful. How important is the sexual side of marriage (Hebrews 13:4)?

# 2. Charles and Sarah Wesley

**How sure should we be? How sure can we be?**

*1. Can love wait?*

Sarah Gwynne had looks and money and interested suitors (p. 29), but she chose to wait for 'the right one' and she was kept waiting. Love is patient (1 Corinthians 13:4). How do you feel about long engagements?

*2. Can love write?*

Sarah and Charles looked forward to receiving their letters (p. 44). Both of them found it easier to express their feelings in writing. What are your feelings or memories about love letters? When is it better to write something to a loved one, and when is it more appropriate or helpful to speak to them?

*3. Can love be sure?*

Sarah knew a great deal about Charles before she ever met him and her patience was rewarded (p. 43). Charles and Sarah waited until they were as sure as they could be. They knew enough about each other to want to spend the rest of their lives together. How important is it to know about your partner? Can you ever really know all about them?

## 4. Can love face up to reality?

Charles's careless attitude about money was fine for him as a bachelor but would have been disastrous for him as a married man. Mrs Gwynne's insistence on a firm financial understanding before marriage was considered wise, and Charles accepted that such things must be talked through and agreed before marriage (p. 44). How important is it to be concerned about financial security, and when is it right to 'take a step of faith'?

## 5. Can love last?

Charles's love for his beautiful Sarah remained and even deepened after smallpox robbed her of her good looks. Looks fade eventually for all of us, but Charles not only assured her of his undying love but declared that this made him love her more than ever for herself (p. 47). How important is physical attraction in marriage?

# 3. William and Catherine Booth

**What is necessary to make a good marriage great?**

1. It takes time – but how much time? William and Catherine's union ripened into a union of heart, purpose and life (p. 63). Marriages, like fruit, need rain as well as sunshine and take time to ripen to full maturity and sweetness.

2. William and Catherine agreed on nearly all the main issues before marriage, but one remained to test them both over several years – the question of the equality of the sexes and women's ministry (p. 64). Male chauvinism and militant feminism will never agree, but different opinions present a wonderful challenge in marriage, and when faced up to and discussed through until agreement is reached leave both parties wiser, humbler, and more in love than before. In the end it took Catherine years of research to settle the matter in her mind, then it took all her courage to enter the pulpit herself, and finally convince William in practice as well as in theory (p. 69). Look up some scriptures on authority and submission in marriage (Ephesians 5:22–28; Colossians 3:18–19).

3. The spirit of romance that flourishes during courtship can and should continue to thrive throughout marriage.

Bramwell Booth said that 'whenever his father came home to Catherine he would be like a lover of twenty come to visit his girl'! How can you keep romance alive in your marriage?

# 4. Smith and Polly Wigglesworth

**How should we resolve problems within marriage?**

1. Smith and Polly were different in so many ways: in temperament, gifts, abilities, and education. Recognition of different roles helps. How do you see the role of the husband and the role of the wife? Do you think they are equal but different and complementary to each other, to make one great couple, and two even greater individuals?

2. Recognising that all marriages – even the best ones – have problems is important. It comes as a shock to many to discover that a great person such as Smith Wigglesworth went through a period of spiritual coldness when he allowed his business to take over his life (p. 83). The problem took two years to overcome, but throughout this period Polly kept her patience and maintained her own spiritual life and her sense of humour, as revealed in the story of Smith pushing her out of the back door and locking it, only for her to return via the unlocked front door. Laughter won when further words may well have proved disastrous (p. 84). What was the secret of her good humour?

3. Change always brings problems, but there is only a problem if we refuse to change. After Smith's visit to Sunderland, it

was Polly's turn to have to face up to change. She had always led the services and done the preaching while Smith had counselled the new converts. They were a great team. To change after many years took real grace, humility and courage, with the result that they both entered into a greater period of blessing (p. 87). What areas of change do you need to face?

4. After Polly's passing, Smith acknowledged how much he owed to her (p. 89). Never be slow to acknowledge how much you owe the one you love. How can you tell them today?

# 5. Billy and Ruth Graham

**Can Christian marriages survive the pressures of modern society?**

*1. Yes – if things are started right.*

Billy and Ruth's first date was at a performance of Handel's *Messiah*, but just sitting next to Ruth set his heart beating faster. He wanted to rush ahead, but he listened when his friends advised caution (p. 94). Marriage cannot and should not be rushed into.

*2. Yes – if the doubts are dealt with correctly beforehand.*

Ruth and Billy had long and earnest discussions, sometimes 'heated' (p. 99). It pays to talk – especially before commitments are made. Silence is not always golden, and sulky silences are destructive. Never let the sun go down on your anger (Ephesians 4:26).

*3. Yes – if you can sometimes agree to differ.*

Billy, having become a Baptist, wanted Ruth to be baptised by total immersion, but Ruth resisted. As a Presbyterian, she could not accept that this was necessary. Further, as Billy was an interdenominational as well as an international evangelist, she felt that retaining her Presbyterianism would help rather than hinder his ministry. In the end, Billy accepted Ruth's position (p. 99). It is important always to respect each other's views and convictions.

### 4. Yes – if you can agree when it is time to end all uncertainty.

When Ruth had a sudden bout of uncertainty, God helped Billy to make Ruth see that there was no longer any room for doubt about their getting married (p. 100). Ruth's commitment and support was total (as seen in that precious letter p. 104), as was her acceptance of Billy's God-given calling as an evangelist – even though she knew it would mean frequent partings.

### 5. Yes – if you always honour each other.

Ruth accepted that her role as a famous evangelist's wife would mean that she was mainly the home-maker, and Billy always appreciated that Ruth was the vital part of his great ministry (p. 106). International fame and honours were never allowed to spoil or intrude on their home and family. Their marriage has withstood all the pressures and temptations that modern society, and lonely nights away from each other, could put upon them.

# 6. Jacob and Rachel

**Can civilised society survive without marriage?**

1. Is marriage God's idea or man's? Marriage was under attack in New Testament times as in our day. Jesus quoted the author of Jacob's story when questioned on the feasibility of marriage as a life-long commitment: 'Haven't you read . . . that at the beginning the Creator "made them male and female", and said, "For this reason a man will leave his father and mother and be united to his wife, and the two will become one flesh"? So they are no longer two, but one' (Matthew 19:4–6/Genesis 2:24). The call of Jesus to go back to the beginning of human relationships constitutes a rock-sure foundation for all prepared to commit themselves to building a life-long union based on biblical principles.

2. The Authorised (King James) Version of the Bible translates this verse as 'shall cleave unto his wife'. The Greek word for cleave means 'to be glued to, be closely bound to'. One may say, therefore, that marriage is not a matter of being stuck with someone, rather it is a matter of sticking together like glue throughout the whole of life, come what may. Despite being tricked into marrying Leah, Jacob remained committed to her,

and God blessed their union, for it was through their descendants that the Messiah would come.

3. What does the Bible say about polygamy? This story highlights the unhappiness of polygamous marriages: it clearly destroyed all sisterly love between Leah and Rachel, as well as creating constant friction between their offspring. The divinely approved ideal is a life-long union between one man and one woman (Genesis 2:24).

4. Isaac sought God's will in choosing his Rebekah, and God blessed their relationship with a deep and meaningful love (Genesis 24:67). Jacob was guided by his parents and he crossed the desert to find a God-fearing wife. Rachel was the love of his life. As F. B. Meyer says when commenting on Genesis 29:18, 'This was clearly a love match. And no marriage is heaven-made, heaven-sent, or heaven-sanctioned which does not spring from a supreme love.'

5. Jacob and Rachel experienced the wonder of lasting love some four thousand years ago. Their love was tested to the limits. Never mind mothers-in-law, just think about having Laban for a father-in-law! The customs and conventions of the marriage ceremony are different today, but not the commitment required, nor our human frailties!

# 7. Colin and Hazel Whittaker

**Ten commandments for a happy marriage**

I felt it was only fair that my precious wife Hazel should have the last word in my book. So I asked her to say what she feels are the secrets of a successful marriage, and here are the key words she rattled off faster than I could write them down.

1. Communication: always keep the lines of communication open, when at home and when away. Be sure to keep in touch with the family at all times.

2. Commitment: be faithful to each other. Never forget you are married, and behave accordingly.

3. Loyalty at all times and in every way is essential and to be expected.

4. Tolerance and forgiveness will always be needed this side of heaven. Sorry is a wonderful word, but be careful how you say it, for even sorry can sound anything but an apology if said in the wrong way.

5. Humour is priceless: never lose your sense of humour.

6. Nurture carefully your sense of equality. Remember that you are joint heirs of the kingdom and 'there is neither . . . slave nor free, male nor female, for you are all one in Christ Jesus' (Galatians 3:28).

7. Appreciation of each other must always be evident. Saying 'I love you' or 'thank you' every day goes a long way.

8. Be sure to have some mutual interests that you can enjoy together, as well as space to be yourselves.

9. Listen and take time to truly appreciate each other's opinions.

10. Be sure to keep romance alive.

# Bibliography

## Martin and Katrina Luther

F. W. Boreham, *A Bunch of Everlastings*, Abingdon Press, Nashville, 1920.

T. M. Lindsay, *Luther and the German Reformation*, T. & T. Clark, Edinburgh, 1900.

A. Skevington Wood, *Captive to the Word*, Paternoster Press, Carlisle, 1969.

John M. Todd, *The Bible in the World* magazine, The Bible Society, Swindon, 1967.

John M. Todd, *Luther – A Life*, Hamish Hamilton, London, 1982.

## Charles and Sarah Wesley

Philip L. Carter, *The New Room and the Wesleys*, The New Room, Bristol, 1984.

Frederick C. Gill, *Charles Wesley: The First Methodist*, Lutterworth Press, Cambridge, 1964.

Percy Livingstone Parker, *John Wesley's Journal* (abridged), Ibister & Co., London, 1902.

John Telford (ed.), *The Journal of Charles Wesley 1736–1739*, Robert Culley, London, 1909.

John Telford, *Wesley's Chapel and Wesley's House*, Charles H. Kelly, London.

Brian Thompson, *Hearts Aflame*, Moorley's Bible and Bookshop, Ilkeston, Derbyshire, 1988.

John Pollock, *Wesley: The Preacher*, Kingsway Publications, Eastbourne, 2000.

A. Skevington Wood, *The Burning Heart – John Wesley, Evangelist*, Paternoster Press, Carlisle, 1976.

John A. Vickers, *Charles Wesley*, Foundery Press, Peterborough, 1990.

## William and Catherine Booth

Harold Begbie, *The Life of William Booth Vols 1 and 2*, Macmillan, London, 1920.

Bramwell Booth, *Echoes and Memories*, Hodder & Stoughton, London, 1925.

Catherine Bramwell Booth, *Catherine Booth: The Story of Her Loves*, Hodder & Stoughton, London, 1970.

Richard Collier, *General Next to God*, Fontana (Collins), London, 1976.

Roger J. Green, *Catherine Booth*, Monarch, Crowborough, 1997.

Charles Ludwig, *Mother of an Army*, Bethany House Publishers, Minnesota, 1988.

## Smith and Polly Wigglesworth

Stanley Howard Frodsham, *Smith Wigglesworth – Apostle of Faith*, Assemblies of God, Luton, 1949.

William Hacking, *Reminiscences of Smith Wigglesworth*, Evangel Press, London, 1972.

Donald Gee, *These Men I Knew*, Assemblies of God, Nottingham, 1980.

Jack Hywel-Davies, *Baptised by Fire: The Life of Smith Wigglesworth*, Hodder & Stoughton, London, 1987.

## Billy and Ruth Graham

Billy Graham, *World Aflame*, Cedar Books, Tadworth, 1968.

Billy Graham, *Just As I Am*, HarperCollins (Marshall Pickering), London, 1997.

Ruth Bell Graham, *It's My Turn*, Hodder & Stoughton, London, 1983.

Ruth Bell Graham, *Prodigals and Those Who Love Them*, Word (UK), Milton Keynes, 1991.

John Pollock, *Billy Graham – Evangelist to the World*, Harper & Row, New York, 1979.

## Jacob and Rachel

F. B. Meyer, *Israel: A Prince with God*, Morgan & Scott, London, 1909.

# Marriage as God Intended

## by Selwyn Hughes

The Bible begins and ends with a marriage. It begins with the account of the marriage of Adam and Eve, and ends with the marriage of the bride ... to Christ the heavenly Bridegroom.

Selwyn Hughes believes that marriage is important to God. As both husband and counsellor he draws on his many years' experience, blending biblical principles with practical suggestions on how to let God keep your marriage at its best. He considers:

- Who is the head of the house?
- How to 'fight' like a Christian
- How to cope with extra-marital attraction
- How to communicate
- Parents and in-laws
- Divorce and remarriage

 Kingsway Publications